There Is a Place on Earth

There Is a
Place on Earth
A Woman in Birkenau

Giuliana Tedeschi

Translated by Tim Parks

Pantheon Books, New York

Library of Congress Cataloging-in-Publication Data

Tedeschi Brunelli, Giuliana.
  [C'è un punto delle terra.   English]
  There is a place on earth. a woman in Birkenau/by Giuliana Tedeschi; translated by Tim Parks.
    p.   cm.
  Translation of: C'è un punto dèlla terra.
  1. Brzezinka (Poland: Concentration camp)
  2. Holocaust, Jewish (1939–1945)—Personal narratives.
  3. Tedeschi Brunelli, Giuliana.   I. Title.
  D805.P7T3813   1992   940.53'18—dc20
                                                  91-34414

ISBN 0-679-40303-5

Book design by M. Kristen Bearse

Manufactured in the United States of America
First American Edition

Contents

1

There Is
a Place on Earth...

There is a place on earth, a desolate heath, where the shadows of the dead are multitudes, where the living are dead, where there is only death, hate, and pain.

Surrounding the place and cutting it off from life are thick walls of darkness by night, and by day the infinity of space, the whistle of the wind, the cawing of crows, the stormy sky, the gray of the stones. You arrive, optimistic, by train after a long ride through the green woods of Bavaria and beside the cool rivers of Moldavia, landscapes you gaze at with the eyes of one who is still a tourist. But once the gate has closed and the barbed wire is behind you, you are in hell.

The people here have dull, dilated eyes, dry and hostile. The new arrivals wait for time to pass and for their own eyes to become inexpressive and clouded, or to close forever from exhaustion and horror.

—

In the hut the lights all came on at once. The voice lashed out at the bunks, sharp and authoritative.

"Aufstehen! Aufstehen!" In the bunks carved out one above the other in the walls, human forms, thickly packed as rabbits in their hutches, lay under rough army blankets. They were women who had arrived the day before from Italy, arrived in Upper Silesia, in Birkenau.

"Aufstehen! Aufstehen und schnell die Betten machen." The voice drew nearer. Goaded, the women sat up, threw back their blankets, and looked around in a daze.

Each was alone, surrounded by strangers, crushed between the two bodies of her unknown companions left and right. They still belonged too much to the world they had left behind, they didn't understand the world they had fallen into, didn't understand that they had lost life's most essential quality, the joy of living. At that moment of brusque awakening, the women felt only one thing with any clarity, their regret for the lost morning hour of drowsy slumber.

There Is a Place on Earth

Through the bright curtains the morning light fills the room with a diffuse glow. You lie on your bed with your eyes half-closed. In your semiconscious state your pupils register the daytime brightness. Then the whole outside world gradually penetrates, takes shape, weight, color, until at some imperceptible moment in the gradual stirring of the senses you find yourself distinct from the things around you, awake.

This state of languor, suspended between dream and reality, this drowning in the infinite and rising to the surface again, escapes the notice of the conscious mind in the rhythm of normal life.

On the night of April 11, 1944, the absence of that state of drowsiness before total awakening, the suddenness of the contact with an inconceivable reality, overwhelmed us all under a wave of nausea. Nausea to find our bodies covered with filthy rags and shapeless garments from which our skin shrank away in goose pimples while a cold shiver ran down our spines. Nausea at the sight of all that awkward, suffering humanity, ragged and dirty, reduced to a flock of huddling beasts.

But there was still one small ray of light, and amid so much squalor hope shone all the more brightly.

"Two, maybe three months and the war will be over . . ." "Two, maybe three months," the men in the world "outside" were saying as they read in their papers of the Russian army's swift, victorious advance across Romania.

"Two, maybe three months . . . the Russians will be at the German border, the English will have made their landing . . . the war will be over." "Two, maybe three months . . ." said the people arriving from France, from Holland, from Belgium. And the prisoners said to themselves, "We must hold on; just two, maybe three months more."

Wakened by the guards' shouting, the women sat up, looked around, lost. They groped about in the mess of clothes and combs and half-eaten crusts of bread where margarine had been spread with a finger. The bread had the rough texture of sawdust. The margarine tasted rancid. No one was hungry. They bustled about pointlessly, desperate and humiliated. Underpants were generally male, had no elastic or ties, wouldn't stay up. Socks slipped down to the ankles, shirts still bore the stains of fleas that had lived on other bodies. Everything generated a sense of disgust and impotence. The bread, wrapped up in your clothes or thrust into pockets or wound in a rag tied to your belt, made your stomach turn. The few who had a piece of a comb would share it with their neighbors.

In our bunks we began to disentangle rumpled hair, picking out stalks of straw that had come from the mattresses. When we put our hands into the warm, living mass of our hair, we realized that the women along the opposite wall were watching us and hurrying to cover their own completely shaved heads with horrible caps and berets. A week before we arrived, no prisoner had been admitted to the camp without having first been brutally deprived of every female grace, every aspect of her femininity.

Despite being bundled up in filthy rags, faces half-hidden and distorted by their caps, all the women in the camp looked young, and some of them were beautiful. When the cry of *"Zählappell"* echoed between the rows of bunks, they all climbed wearily down, holding on to the edge of their beds and pushing their toes between the bricks of the wall. Chased outside with shoves and shouts like a flock of sheep, the women huddled together, looking for the familiar faces of those who had been next to them in the bunks.

Outside they found the huge darkness of the night. A lamp over the door to the hut cast an uncertain glow. A row of dark, becapped ghosts was formed. Again, one's spirit was shaken by a tremor of grim foreboding. In the utter silence and dark light, the silhouettes of the other huts stood out. Row upon row of huts, all the same, hundreds of other dark shadows lined up before them. The place might have been tossed up that very night from the bowels of the earth, the way a volcano erupting at night can change a whole landscape; or it might have been the product of some haunted imagination: unique, unrepeatable, out of this world.

No voices or noises reached the place, only the lacerating, spasmodic wail of a train fading away in the darkness in dispiriting echo. The cold bit into hands and feet, shoulder blades shook and shuddered with nervousness. The muscles in your back ached and shivers ran right down to your waist.

Three big steaming wooden tubs appeared, each carried by four women prisoners. Enameled iron mess tins full of scalding tea were passed along the first row. Each tin had to do for five prisoners. With a sense of repugnance we laid our lips against the rim of the common tin. Two or three mouthfuls of the bitter liquid was as much as you could manage. This and the same thing in the afternoon were all we would have to drink all day. There was no drinking water. How long did those black ghosts stand there rigid in their rows? Maybe an hour, maybe two hours . . . how could one know when there was nothing to evoke the convention of time?

When you went back into the huts, dawn was just beginning to break.

"You know," said a voice, "what time they woke us? Half past three."

2

Quarantine
in
Block 13

Time moves slowly when life has been reduced to
the animal essentials. No one was allowed to leave
the quarantine block or to move from their bunks.
The hours were passed waiting for the big moments
of the day: the roll call before dawn and at sundown, soup, tea, going to the toilets, the bread
handout.

Soup is served in a single mess tin for five or six
—a dishwater broth of stringy yellow turnips with
a very occasional piece of potato or carrot. With no
spoons the women bent over the common tin like
dogs around a bowl.

Two or three mouthfuls sucked up in turns, and our sense of disgust for this animal way of eating is even greater than our repugnance for the contents.

The bread is handed out; portions are weighed in the prisoners' hands, compared with other portions. Your stomach craving, your eye measures the little blocks of margarine meanly cut by the *bloccova** and her helpers who speculate on the prisoners' rations.

You didn't go to the toilet because you personally needed to; the *bloccova* took you there in groups when she felt like it. The latrine hut was crowded, you could barely get in. Running down the middle was a raised cement platform with holes at regular intervals along both sides. Sitting on the platform were ghosts of women, with other women in the same position beside and behind, and all of them pushed and shoved by yet other waiting women who were standing. From the raised dresses of the seated women emerged emaciated, skeletal bodies, the skin sinking deep into fearful hollows, legs no longer able to hold the bust up straight, festering with boils, eruptions of avitaminosis, scabies. How long would it be before we were reduced to the same state! On the rough faces of Russians and Poles and the coarse features of peasants from the Ukraine and the Polish hills, a tragic absence of humanity showed itself in outbreaks of savagery.

* The *bloccova* was the fellow-inmate assigned by the SS with responsibility for the barracks, or *Block* (German).

There Is a Place on Earth

You had at last managed to find a place on the platform when a big Polish woman would heave you from your seat with a threatening shout of *"Schweine Jüdin!"* and truculently take your place.

These beings were everywhere in the camp, they had been given certain jobs to do, they would appear outside your window, they would hang around the huts, stumble along the roads. It was as if the soul gradually withdrew from these relics, disdained the body, now inert and passive, that nature had assigned it.

In the hours when there was nothing to do, memories of the world left behind would come flooding back, and with them the need to get close to your fellow sufferers, to weep with them and hope with them. The bunks of the Italians who had arrived with the April train were all close to each other: eighty young women had been admitted to the camp.

The men had been separated from the women when we got out of the train and sent off to a men's camp; the older people had been loaded into trucks and nobody had seen or heard of them again. In those long unnerving hours waiting for something unexpected, something new to happen, the women got to know each other, talked about themselves, learned to appreciate each other.

So I discovered Zilly's hand, a small, warm hand, modest and patient, which held mine in the evening, which pulled up the blankets around my shoulders, while a calm, motherly voice whispered in my ear, "Good night, dear—I have a daughter your age!" And sleep crept slowly into my being along with the trust that hand communicated, like blood flowing along the veins.

So I came across Olga one day and we hid ourselves away together in a corner of the hut. I suddenly felt I would be able to speak to her and she would understand. I spoke about the Dionysian sense of life and she of the spirit and the body. My pupils lost themselves in the whites of her eyes. The huts disappeared, we forgot the barbed wire, and an unbounded liberty of spirit intoxicated us beyond any limit imposed by human bestiality. We decided to be friends.

In scraps and fragments the life of each prisoner entered and mingled with the lives of all the others in confused tales full of gaps. Everyone began with her own story, always the same story of escapes, scares, mistakes, illusions, betrayals, arrests, deportations. Tery had been caught at the Swiss border with her husband. Another hour and they would have been safe! Dina, a German, had been living as a refugee in Italy; when the good old days when foreigners could sit and play cards with the police came to an end, she had finally been arrested together with her father. Gerty, a small Austrian woman, another who had fled to Italy, had arrived at Auschwitz with her whole family: mother, father, brothers and sisters. Olga had been arrested while traveling because her suitcase was full of books in English and French; suspected of being a spy (why

else would anyone want to read foreign books?),
they had kept her in prison when they discovered
she was a Jew. And there were others, dozens,
hundreds of others, whose lives had unfolded thus
far in all kinds of different experiences, and who
now found themselves brought together in the
same desolate existence of the torture camps.

Before each of us yawned, dark and desperately
seductive, the abyss of one's self; deep inside, with
the uncertainty of images reflected in water, the
faces of parents, husbands, and children appeared,
disappeared, and were superimposed over each
other, and our eyes swelled with tears, our vision
blurred. Then we would be tearing our hearts out,
we would flee from those faces, chase away those
memories in terror, and at the same time we would
hear, rising from the fearful emptiness inside us,
from our terrible loneliness, a long cry of desperation.

Older prisoners had been put in charge of the
sleeping quarters, the blocks, the working parties:
they were the few who had survived, outliving mil-
lions of their countrywomen; they had lost families
and friends, they had seen their fellow prisoners
die in droves amid unspeakable sufferings, appalling horrors. Their eyes were hard but would occa-
sionally light up with flashes of madness and
aberration. The Germans could count on them.
Having grown old in an atmosphere of hate and
brutality, they would never have shown the slight-
est mercy to the prisoners under them. They hated

those who had suffered less than themselves, those who had arrived in the camps after them.

These women, the *bloccova* and *stubova*,* were necessary for putting into practice the perpetual torture that was life in the camps.

The emptiness grows inside you and seems to drown every desire to live. The cry rising from deep in your being sticks in your throat and chokes your breathing; tears veil your eyes, there is no answer to the whys of your desperation, and a heartbreaking yearning for the past fastens its powerful tentacles around your soul. At such moments an order, a blow, the hardness of another's eyes, annihilate your interior world, impose as essential a reality whose meaning or logic you can never unravel. One minute it's the mad torment of the bed-making, being forced to arrange your blankets meticulously over thin straw mattresses full of holes; next it's the imposition of having to spend all day sitting on your bunk but without ever leaning back on your mattress where human patience and endurance have already been pushed to the limit in your attempts to spread the blankets without a single wrinkle; and then there was the crazy system for cleaning the sleeping quarters.

When nobody has a name, it's so easy to say, *"Wo ist die Schwarze? Schwarze, komm her!"* Amid a

* The *stubova* was the fellow-inmate charged by the SS with responsibility for the prisoners of a barrack-room, or *Stube* (German).

12

sea of faces, all of the same complexion, the fact that you have dark skin and dark hair condemns you to a whole range of chores. Somebody thrusts a brush into your hand and you have to sweep the floor inch by inch. When your back is beginning to ache, the *stubova* in charge of the dormitory hurls four or five buckets of water across the floor. "Wash it!" And crawling about wearily with your rag, you have to mop up every last drop. When you're finished, you're panting hard, your eyes turn to your bunk, your safe little den, but inexorably more and more buckets are emptied across the floor under a stony gaze.

You get back to your mattress, bent double, staggering; something human has been lost from the expression on your face, the coordination of your limbs, the depths of your soul. What minimal intellectual capacity you still have grasps hold of this truth: if you are to get tougher, if you are to survive, if you are to achieve some miraculous reconquest of the intellect, you will have to become a brute.

—

Quarantine Hut 13, Camp A, was full. With the arrival of a trainload of Greeks, a thousand women filled all the bunks carved into the walls and, paler, blanker, more desperate every day, a thousand faces looked out over the edge of their mattresses. The air was stale, and where the breeze from outside penetrated one of the rare holes in the wall, women would be gasping for it in short, panting breaths, chests heaving. The groups sat apart in silence. Immersed in her own spiritual isolation, each prisoner was nevertheless condemned to awareness of the physical presence of her neighbors to left or right, bodies inevitably touching, squeezed together in that inconceivably small space. The few words that were murmured, short sentences, muttered stories, were indistinguishable against the insistent, muffled background noise, like the echo of a seashell held to your ear.

"Good news, girls!" Gerty's voice announced, her pale, freckled face appearing over the edge of the bed. With a quick pull of her arms she lifted herself up, sat down, slipped off a pair of heavy shoes without laces and hid them carefully under her mattress.

Her nearest neighbors huddled round her.

"What's she saying?" asked the women farther away, heads turning.

Gerty was only sixteen. She'd been born in Vienna but at four years old had already known the meaning of that strange term "stateless person," a definition applying to an ever-larger multitude of refugees.

Flight and exile began when she was twelve; four years of obscure, modest, patient survival in Italy, remembering the old safe carefree Vienna, hoping for a new Vienna that would be welcoming and prosperous. Her father worked as a carpenter, the children grew up, her mother kept the vagrant family above water, patching clothes and making sure there was always stew enough in the pot for five hungry mouths. Arrest and deportation came suddenly and almost inexplicably. But with her knowledge of German, Gerty had an advantage in camp life.

"I sneaked out to the toilets . . ." she was saying, and the word "toilets" attracted everybody's attention. A certain reverence was reserved for the very name of that great mine of news and information, source of the most amazing rumors, which would spread with incredible speed in every language and to the most out-of-the-way corners of the camp. "Did you know that . . . *Mes enfants, on dit que . . . Ecoutez, je l'ai entendu tout à l'heure au cabinet . . .*"

"I spoke to a Pole," Gerty went on, her pale, thoughtful adolescent's face, with its loose straight hair, growing slightly excited. "She says there is a family camp! The mothers, children, and old people live there. One day they sent her to do a job a long way away, outside the fence, and she saw the barbed wire of another camp with women and children around the huts . . ."

"Then our mothers must be there too," breathed Nina, and her round face flushed with hope. The wavy blond fringe that fell unkempt over her forehead (the mop of hair behind had been cropped close like a boy's on arrival in the camp) gave her a girlish look, but her eyes had a bewildered expression as they seemed to gaze obstinately after her mother, remembering how she had walked away when the trainload was sorted, supporting the visibly pregnant elder daughter on her arm.

"We'll meet up again, girls, we'll see our mothers again," said someone who needed to convince the others to convince herself.

"Maybe in the other camp they're better off, probably it's not a labor camp. The mothers look after the children and the old women knit . . . socks and sweaters for the soldiers . . . the Germans must need things like that." Thus daydreamed Alma, who had watched as her mother, a small, thin, frail old woman, had barely been able to climb onto the truck. A breath of hope transformed the girls' faces. It was easy for them to imagine a mother's busy hands working nimbly at her knitting while the little children ran around outside.

—

Along the opposite wall two of the bunks in the first row were taken up by unusual occupants. On the first was a tall, very dark woman with long black arched eyebrows, black eyes, and a wide mouth. Bedraggled, untidily dressed. Around her slack, grayish breasts, visible among the rags left carelessly open on her chest, a bad-tempered ten-month-old baby groped busily. Every now and then the little mouth came off the nipple and two little hands thrust it away in anger. The child cried and the silent mother let her empty breast hang loose outside her dress. Next to her, wrapped in rags and blankets, two other children, aged three and five, nestled like puppies snuggling around a bitch in a kennel. They didn't cry, they faded away—lifeless and cheerless, with no toys, no air, no light.

In the other bunk two sisters, mothers of three children, slowly and carefully sliced up their bread ration, hiding behind the miserliness with which they allotted the food the desperate question "And after this, what next?" The children were all the fruit of mixed marriages; the mothers were "Aryans."

"I got off the train," explained the tall, dark woman, "into a crowd of people, all exhausted, disheveled, afraid. 'Juden Kinder und Weiber!' yelled a German soldier. I was struck by the tone of voice. With the baby asleep in my arm, the children holding my hand, I walked out among the heaps of luggage piled up in front of the train. The other two mothers followed me. 'We're Aryans, the children are mixed,' we said one after the other, breathless, 'the children are mixed, they're baptized.' In the general chaos and confusion an SS man with a skull on his beret listened. He spoke to somebody else, ordered us sharply to change groups, and we came here."

—

I was walking up the narrow corridor between the bunks; the children's bunk was on the left. My steps were slow and unsure in oversized shoes with wooden soles. I saw the dark shadow of the mother bent over a heap of filthy rags wrapped around the baby's puny legs, and a serious, already adult expression in the eyes of the other children. The agonizing desire to take the baby in my arms, to bring his tender cheek to my own, to feel his little hands on my face, was stifled by a sharp pain that seemed to paralyze my heart in my breast. I turned. With ferocious determination I kept my balance on the uneven bricks, put my hands on the edge of my bunk, and lifted myself up as fast as I could. My body fell in a heap, suddenly empty, on the inviolable mattress, the misery of its half-empty sack hidden beneath the wrinkle-free spread of the blankets. My own younger baby girl was in her cot, pink with sleep, her gaze radiant, as if seeing beyond the room, the tips of her thin soft hair turned back on themselves in a first hint of curls on her little head. Through the frosted glass of the bedroom door, visible in filtered light from the corridor, appeared the silhouette of the visored cap of the SS man. Then voices, steps, commotion, questions, denials, desperation.

Nothing in my mind more sharply etched, more lasting than that split-second image, followed by the echo of my suffocated cry in the pillows, "The Germans!"

In her little bed my other little girl's blue eyes widened and darkened with fear. "Mummy, come back soon."

When I realized I was weeping desperately, I felt Zilly's hand on my shoulder, a soft, warm hand that did not tremble, and her voice: "Just think that your children are safe, they've got food to eat . . ."

There Is a Place on Earth

—

The steaming broth tins had nearly reached the last bunks. The confused background noise of the hut had faded as greedy mouths bent over the bowls, but even as they did so, exhaustion was already stifling the vital life spark in dull eyes. The last ten hands stretched out, strength slipping away from frail wrists and hearts beating hollow in their breasts. But the broth was left untouched, steaming and thickening in the tin; for with the fury of a gust of wind a shout now startled the whole hut *"Block dreizehn, baden!"*

Outside, the sharp air brought a sense of relief to the lungs. The showers were situated at the edge of the quarantine camp in a long brick building above which three chimneys constantly belched black smoke.

To get to them we had to cross the whole camp, and our dazed eyes looked around and gazed. It was the first time we had seen the world about us in daylight.

To the right, a row of gray wooden huts formed the *Revier*, the hospital; opposite the showers was an identical building with smoking chimneys and heavy iron bins around the door, the kitchen. A stench of turnips turned the stomach. In gray stone, at regular intervals, the rows of huts stretched away as far as the eye could see, with a high tension barbed-wire fence closing off the horizon in the spaces between. Not a tree, not a blade of grass; no color, no movement.

19

On the opposite side of the roadway a young
woman walked quickly by, hands thrust into the
pockets of a white gown. She wasn't wearing the
usual cap and her hair fell freely in black curls on
the nape of her neck. Easygoing and unaffected, her
body showed signs of outward concessions to
human dignity—the long hair, the shoes that
formed a pair and fitted her feet. She was an Italian
prisoner who had arrived in the camp two months
ago. She worked as a doctor in the hospital. Our
column was marching in rows of five, the Italians
turned to look at her and several hands were raised
in greeting.

Luciana came across the road and caught up with
the column at the door to the showers.

"How's it going, girls, getting used to it? Her
eyes were slightly bloodshot and strangely bright,
and as she spoke, quickly and too casually, she
couldn't prevent the corners of her mouth from
twitching under the pressure of some intense emotion.

"Lucky so and so," Olga immediately thought.
"She's got shoes, she can walk; I either lose mine
or I fall over."

"Please, have you got any cotton," said another,
grabbing her arm, "get me some cotton."

"Cotton"—Luciana laughed ironically—"you
must be joking. You know what we use for ban-
dages here? Paper! Pick up some rags, in the road,
in the mud . . . next month you won't need anything
anyway . . ."

All along I was gazing into her eyes.

"Tell me what's wrong," I said.

"Nothing." Luciana was evasive. She turned to the others near us and smiled: "So, do you like turnips?"

"Tell me," I insisted quietly. "Tell me everything."

Her eyes filled with tears. Her lips trembled. In an almost strangled voice she whispered in my ear, "Selection at the hospital."

"When? How many?" My throat was suddenly dry, my voice wouldn't come.

"This morning. Almost everybody, more than four hundred!"

My heart stopped for a moment and my knees trembled. Did every hut, every nook and cranny, every enigmatic building, the showers, the hospitals, hide a trap? Was death lying in wait everywhere from one end of the camp to the other, within the circle of barbed wire?

"This morning," I repeated, terrified. "Fourteen of our group went into the *Revier*. Them too?"

Luciana was aghast. "How stupid, to go to the hospital as soon as they get here, just because they've got a bit of a sore throat! I told you, 'Don't go to the hospital, work, work for as long as you can.' When you arrived, I came straight to the showers to tell you . . ." She wrung her hands nervously.

Then she calmed down. "There's hasn't been one for three months. Everybody thought, 'Things are getting better. The Germans are nearly finished and they're afraid. See? They're not even cutting people's hair anymore.' They didn't cut your hair. So much for things getting better!"

I realized that to look for some logic behind what happened in the camp would be to go out of your mind.

"Listen"—I felt a need to have done with all doubts, all hopes—"the mothers with babies and the old people who climbed into the trucks when we arrived . . . them too?"

Luciana chose to be ruthless with my still innocent soul, the all-too-visible emotion of my tearful eyes.

"Every trainload," she said brutally, "is decimated on arrival. But we haven't seen the ovens burn for your lot yet . . . What that means, I don't know."

And she hurried off brusquely as the shower doors were thrown open and the first women rushed in.

—

Everybody had their coat spread out around their feet, and one by one dropped their clothes onto it. The windows had no glass in them and the freezing air that rushed in turned skin to gooseflesh and stung our breasts. There were two doors opposite each other that would open at the same time, swinging on their hinges, so that sudden drafts would slice into your shoulders and back like sharp blades. We all stopped looking at each other, eyes dropping down from our defenseless nudity to the bundle of rags below; with no pockets to hide in, one's hands became two heavy independent entities.

To hide ourselves we clutched our bundles of clothes to our breasts and crotches, while each separate limb seemed a painful encumbrance.

Only later, protected by a veil of water and steam and encouraged by the warmth, did we raise our faces, to be overcome once again by disgust.

Bodies, bodies, bodies, many unattractive, many no longer young, some flabby and limp, most imperfect, disproportioned. Crude mass. We all belong to this flesh heap, and we all feel alien to it.

A woman, struck by an epileptic fit, lies sideways on the ground. No one goes to help her. Naked body, anonymous, preserving in its contortions something miserably obscene and gross. Against the whiteness of her flesh, her camp number stands out sharply on her left arm, black figures that have become part of that body now, intimately bound up with its identity. I remembered the needle penetrating my own skin, to leave, dot by dot, the five-figure number 76847, underlined by the triangle symbolizing *Jude*. And I remembered hearing my voice ask: *"Ceci pour toute la vie?"* Since that number was tattooed on my arm, I had learned many things: that what they wrote on the walls of the showers—HALTE DICH SAUBER?; EINE LAUS IST DEIN TOD!—were ironic idiocies, that reality lay in the shove you got from the uniformed German woman who herded you out of the showers still dripping wet into a freezing room without glass in the windows; it lay in the belt of the ambiguous creature watching over us, with her matching skirt and jacket, tie, man's haircut, big boots, and hoarse, unpleasant voice, again like a man's, a drunk's; I learned in short that everything was achieved through the systematic organization of disorganization, with the intention of extinguishing our lives.

3

Arbeit
Macht Frei

It was the Germans' intention that a camp should look like a building site. In the ditches dug between the rows of huts for laying down pipes, hundreds of women moved about with mattocks and picks.

How could these women stick at this from six in the morning to five in the afternoon, on their feet all day, lifting a heavy spade or pick dozens and dozens of times?

And why, just when the war was about to end (wasn't it supposed to be over in two, maybe three months?), were the Germans putting down pipes?

Not to improve life for the prisoners, that's for sure. So? The Russians were expected to arrive from over that way. They might even arrive fairly soon: their advance across Romania had been devastating.

"The Germans," the prisoners daydreamed, "won't want the civilized world to find out how the prisoners in the concentration camps in Poland and Germany really lived, or rather died . . ."

Farther away, near the gate that separated Camp A from Camp B, a small line had been laid to carry freight wagons. Standing by a great heap of sand, a group of women were busily loading it onto the wagons; other women were pushing the wagons and then unloading them at the end of the line.

"Are the wagons heavy? Will we manage it?" the newcomers asked themselves.

There were different jobs, but the women doing them were all the same: mute, gloomy, gray, as though outside of time, in motion since pain was created.

The line of moving wagons met a column of women in rows of five; a female voice spoke in French from the wagons: *"Allô, Madeleine, qu'est-ce que tu fais?"*

Each prisoner in the column had a big block of granite in her arms.

"Tu ne le vois pas? J'amène des pierres," answered another voice behind its stone.

"What are you building?"

The other laughed. *"Tu es bête, chérie!* We're carrying the stones over there to the other side of

the camp, and tomorrow we'll be taking them back
to where they were before. There is no more work,
the Germans are through!"

"*Il y aura toujours des pierres en Pologne, mes
enfants,*" answered the first woman. "*Evidemment,
moi, je ne travaille pas pour la guerre!*"

Come the evening Madeleine wasn't smiling
anymore; all the women were dragging their heels,
walking slowly, clutching the stones to their
breasts. Their faces were worn-out, their ankles
swollen, their backs broken; their ovaries ached.
The headscarves they wore were askew, their
dresses full of dust. But on returning to their huts
after work, they would find written in black letters
on the white central wall: ARBEIT MACHT FREI—
WORK MAKES YOU FREE.

—

After the roll call one morning during the quarantine period, something new happened. They began
to recruit people for work from our camp too, Camp
A, the quarantine camp. The working party leaders
arrived in striped uniforms and recruited forty or
fifty women for a particular job. On their chests beside their numbers, instead of the Star of David,
these leaders had a black triangle, the symbol for
German prostitutes interned in the work camps as a
punishment. In the camp they enjoyed the privilege of being feared and respected. From the low-
est level of human society they had gone to the top
levels of camp society. Our nerves were tense: this
was the beginning of a new phase and one we

27

feared; secretly, we armed ourselves with dumb, passive resistance. Under the Germans work was a form of persecution, and all the prisoners could do was save their energy in every way possible.

Those chosen marched off while the women left behind to the boredom of their bunks felt sorry for their companions and could barely believe their own good luck.

"But where's Tery?" some were asking, congratulating themselves on the pleasant warmth of their bunks. Tery had been among those chosen.

"Yes, Tery!" said Zilly, and some of the others confirmed, "Yes, her!" But what would Tery do on her own? With those trembling, dilated pupils in her scared face? An infant terror beyond all reason was apparent in every gesture of her withered woman's body—in her wobbly trembling limbs, her hoarse, slightly squeaky voice, a way she had of constantly whining her self-pity. "I'll die here, I'll never make it . . ." Her fellow prisoners would look on, seeing thin hair over sunken temples and high round forehead, frail legs and arms, a flat chest, slightly bent shoulders.

They lowered their heads. "She'll never make it . . . never make it . . ." And they were moved by the thought of the nine-year-old boy, only child of a late marriage, waiting for his mother in Switzerland. ". . . and if I never go back, you must tell him," Tery went on, "how very much his mummy loved him." The tears flowed slowly down her faded cheeks from eyes that were never dry.

Her fellow prisoners were overcome by her tenderness and sensitivity, the intensity of her suffering; but soon they began to feel slightly irritated. They wanted to be strong, to resist, and nothing is more contagious than tenderness, memories, sentiment; sometimes their pity would change to resentment.

"She's always moaning and complaining, as if we weren't suffering the same things she is . . ."

"She cries and despairs, as if we didn't have children and husbands far away . . ."

So Tery worked that day, digging trenches for the pipes. She worked the next day and the next. She wasn't smart enough to think of some trick for getting out of it. She didn't hide in the toilets, didn't drop her shovel in the ditch, risk a belting for the sake of a few minutes' rest. Her theory was: "We mustn't make the Germans angry; please, don't let's make them angry!" Instinctively willing as she was to bend before any blows, to recoil from any confrontation, her back simply attracted contempt and beatings, ached with weariness. And one day a prisoner who cared for her and worked next to her, saw her sink to her knees, hands held high, punished in front of the whole hut by the ruthless eighteen-year-old *bloccova*.

Her expression was sickening—full of desperation and contrition instead of hatred and disdain.

—

The bunk behind was empty; the girls had all been recruited and sent off to work. In crept a thin, shivering shadow, flattening itself against boards and mattress. The body was as though crumpled inside a light faded coat in a gesture of resignation and surrender.

"I ran for it," little Tea told her companions. "The sacks of cement were too heavy. And I'm cold; at roll call my shoulders were aching. Look at the clothes they gave me: a dress with short sleeves, a flimsy coat with no lining." She must have had a fever and kept rubbing her hand against her burning forehead and flushed cheeks. "Anyway, I'd rather die. Mummy must be dead too by now." Tea spoke in the calm voice of someone who has thought things through and made up her mind.

Coming back from work, the other women bent down to speak to her. They were more talkative: they had seen meadows and trees outside the camp, the train a couple of miles away; they had seen other work parties and the men. The men. Perhaps one day they would see their men, the men from their train . . . And stretching themselves out wearily on pallets that only partly covered the boards beneath, they were less aware than usual how hard and inhospitable they were. "Another day done with," they all thought, taking heart. "I've survived the work ordeal. I didn't think I'd make it. Now I know that maybe I will . . ."

—

She knew she would see him. At a certain point the field rose slightly. At the bottom of the slope there were hundreds of squared-off clods of dirt. The women reached the place in line, took two grassy clods each in their arms and set off one after the other along the same path they had taken the day before. They had to cross two huge fields and take the clods to a camp far away.

"Stay as far to the side as possible," one prisoner told her. "He was there yesterday. There, see that group of men over there? They're digging a trench. We'll be quite near them and you'll see him. But watch it, you're not supposed to talk to the men."

They set off—the friend in front, Mansi behind. When the men saw the women walking by only a few yards away, they lifted their heads slightly and raised their eyes beneath lowered eyelids.

He saw his wife and his pick hung in midair. She was still beautiful, he thought, even beneath clothes that fell gracelessly to her feet. A handkerchief tied under her chin covered her head and shaded her forehead a little. The mass of wavy blond hair had gone, but the sharp profile had something more spiritual about it and her eyes had kept their intense mountain-lake blue.

Their eyes met, they gazed at each other, brought their whole souls together, their lips parted without saying a word. The pick came down on the ground again, the woman walked slowly by. Her gait was light, swaying, it didn't seem she could be wearing heavy wooden clogs. Her heart had stopped for a moment but now began to beat hard, her feet started to hurry. She caught up with her companions. She knew now that when they came back she would see him again. When she came back, she would be behind him, she would speak to him.

He knew it was her voice but didn't turn immediately. He waited till he was bent down before looking at her. She had already passed and he saw her tall, elegant figure. He thought how she was like one of those thin, pliant saplings you can't snap.

Again, the line of women with their clods appeared in the distance. It was he who spoke first.

"Hang on. Don't despair, we've got to make it . . . to get home . . . I think of you all the time. Now I've seen you I could work six hours longer and eat a slice of bread less . . ."

Under the tender, intense gaze of her husband, the woman felt her strength grow. She began to believe they really would make it home. For four long journeys her feet hurried until they reached the place where he was, then slowed down, trembled, then speeded up again. Her arms felt strong and the clods light until she reached the men, then all of a sudden, when she'd passed them, the clods weighed heavily and her arms grew tired.

Something had changed in her; her movements and gestures had taken on a confidence and calm alien to the rest of us; her eyes had that fixed, solemn, serene look of someone concentrating more on what is inside than what is outside.

"If we get back to Italy," she told me one evening, calmly eating her bread, "I want to have a child. I did have a tiny, tiny baby, but he died . . ." She was the only one who didn't seem to notice how swollen her legs were getting from all the walking, how bitter and rough the bread was against the tongue.

Every evening I shouted to her from my bunk: "Did you see him? Any news?" And I would be saying over and over to myself: "God, let me see my husband one day, like she has!"

But one evening I sensed I mustn't ask her anything. She was lying down, her bread uneaten by her pillow. Another woman told me, "The men didn't come today. They sent them to work somewhere else."

—

The women who hadn't as yet been assigned to their provisional jobs were used for the *Rollkommando*.

Two carts with barrels would be waiting for them in the morning behind the huts. The prisoners grabbed hold of the rickety drawbar and side struts, and the creaking cart—its barrel not properly closed, its revolting contents spewing out—was set in motion and heaved toward the camp gate. At the SS checkpoint the cart was stopped and the prisoners formed a group for a quick head-count. Then, escorted by an armed *Posten* with a German shepherd, or by a swaggering *Aufseherin*, they set off again out into the country. The task inevitably brought with it a strong sense of humiliation, but everybody soon got over that. The hurried run with the cart, even in our torn shoes or heavy clogs, brought a healthy sense of physical excitement, and there before our eyes, giving us the attractive illusion of freedom, was the country and the sky, the boundless horizon.

Along the road the crust of asphalt had split open in holes, hollows, and cracks. On rainy days the whole thing was a bog, and our feet slithered or got stuck in the slippery sludge.

After a quarter of an hour's trot from the camp, a path forked off the main road and ran down to the left. This was where we had to steer the carts and it took a tricky maneuver with the drawbar to make sure that the wheels didn't lose speed and sink under the weight of their load into the soft ground. Halfway down the path, near a low embankment, was a line of pits where the carts' contents were to be poured.

A working party of Polish men had been given the task of emptying the cart, and this meant the women could take a break.

We looked around. The countryside was somewhat bleak, with hardly any trees, the railway line running along the horizon. "Over there are the Russians, the ones we're waiting for . . . over there is the Italy we left behind," said the women, getting their bearings. If the railway brought wagons full of crashed planes, broken wings, twisted nose cones, heading back to Germany, then hearts lifted in secret hope; if the trains ran toward the front with wagons full of brand-new trucks all carefully lined up, our fear that the Germans would be able to hold out returned.

There Is a Place on Earth

When the sky was blue, if you half-closed your eyes and intensified the colors, enriched the land's fertility with nostalgia and imagination, then you could see Italy. At moments like this, having checked out the *Posten*'s expression, we would try to get close to the earth: we'd lie down, heads resting on the grassy soil, and enjoy losing ourselves in its living embrace.

But often the sky was dense with huge gray and white clouds. Blown by the wind, they hurried on their way like wild horses. That was Poland! The rain would begin to fall, unrelenting, sometimes irksomely thin and penetrating, sometimes tumbling in heavy showers. Why was God taking it out on us too? In the small hut, whose chimney gave off a thread of smoke (doubtless there was a stove in there and some nice tea), the *Aufseherin* with her black triangle would be chatting with the *Posten* or the leader of the men's party.

Outside on the soaking soft grass, mute, patient, stiffening creatures exposed to the inclemency of both nature and man arranged themselves to form a block, shoulder-to-shoulder, breast-to-breast.

When the rain had finally stopped or eased off, we were allowed to set off back. Zilly took her place at the central bar of the cart: surrounded by friends, she could pretend to pull while in fact only taking care to run without stumbling, no easy task for someone her age.

Bianca Maria ran at the head of the drawbar, pulling with renewed energy. Her slim figure stretched forward; her silken gray eyes, fruit of the Russian blood that ran in her veins, lit up and from her lips would come the Polish cry *"Dalej, dalej*—on, on!" Thus she helped us to drag the much heavier cart of our captivity.

—

When the sky is gray, the huts are gray, the roads are gray, and you yourself feel you are being absorbed more and more into the environment, there is nothing in the outside world that reaches you or brings a ray of warmth. In the middle of a path between the huts stood a cart with high sides and a long drawbar full of trash and waste from the kitchen. Women in striped uniforms with the red triangle of the "politicals" were already in their places, trying to drag it on their own.

"Hey, girls, the thing don't wanna budge this morning!" I heard to my surprise, as I, Olga, and some others were approaching to make up the working party's number.

Spoken in a Lombardy dialect, the words brought us close to home and in a warm hug, hanging on to the cart, we all felt less alone.

"Ah"—Ginetta sighed—"when we get back to Italy!" Grabbing the drawbar, she struggled to keep the cart pointing in the right direction. She had a fine open face, a frank smile.

"Shut up, shut up, filthy goddamned Germans," said another with a spare, dry face.

"Why are you here?" I asked the one nearest to me.

There Is a Place on Earth

"Oh, strikers!" said the woman with the thin face. "That's their story. One morning they come into the factory: 'Come on, who wants to go to a meeting?' Fifty of us go. When we get back, they tell us, 'You've been on strike, you're under arrest.' Prison, then deportation. Understand, they had to keep the SS happy. Somebody had to have been on strike in every factory and everybody had to know that the strikers had been arrested . . . ."

"All lies! There's one in our hut," said Ginetta, "Maria . . . Cries all the time, she left a ten-month-old baby behind her. She hadn't been working in the factory for a year. They went to get her at home . . . striker . . . And you?" she added, looking at me and Olga, "why are you here?"

"Jews." The three of them looked at us.

"The way I see it," said the third, who hadn't spoken yet, "the Jews I knew were all all right. They worked and looked after their kids. People like us in the end."

One of the cart's wheels sank into a hole in the ground. We all dug our feet in and thrust with arms and legs to get the thing moving again as soon as possible. Already the German *Aufseherin* was shouting, *"Weiter, weiter, los!"*

"The hell with you," muttered the one with the lean face. All at once I felt the German wasn't human at all but a mere robot in comparison with these working women with their serene, consolatory wisdom. And I sensed that they were stronger than I was. It was their freedom from any of those tortuous problems to do with one's personality;

37

they had an innate defense mechanism. And I felt an enormous desire for their company, and a sense of calm from this contact with their simple, generous natures.

"Doesn't matter, girls," Olga was saying, "we'll be back, and soon. And we'll all get together by Lake Lecco . . ."

We had crossed the entire field; but on the track leading to the gate we had to stop. Two girls holding a *Trage*, a wooden plank with two carrying poles often used for transporting potatoes or stones, were coming toward us.

Their load had been covered with a filthy, torn blanket. But the blanket was too short. A yellow, skeletal leg with a callused foot swung loose in front; to one side a stiff hand stuck out. Under the blanket the body still had the attitude of its last death throes. The girls walked straight ahead, swinging the *Trage* between them. They were thinking of something else, talking about something else, and they didn't bother to check their load.

They put the *Trage* on the ground. The body rocked as if made of wood; the leg and the arm hit the ground. Then they changed places and calmly went on their way. Olga spat twice and twisted her foot into the ground. I was overtaken by nausea and a desire to vomit.

"Hadn't you ever seen anyone dead?" whispered Olga.

"Never." and I said: "I wonder if the real dead" —by which I meant those in their beds, with candles, flowers, and arms crossed on their breasts—"I wonder if they will make any impression after this."

"Maybe they will," she said.

I remembered, from way back in my childhood, my emotion at the sight of candles seen through a dark window, my vague fear of one day having to see a lifeless human being for the first time, and my feeling of respectful reverence toward death and bereavement.

All gone. I pressed my hand into my stomach out of horror and revulsion.

—

One morning we found the carts empty. The men who were supposed to fill them had been taken away for other jobs. So now we would have to do the most unpleasant part of the work as well as the rest. The pit we had to go to was located inside the hospital area. The ground was pitted with holes and the cart had to be taken in with an energetic swerve to get over the uneven ground. Clutching the sides, we ran through the gate.

"Look, there's Vigevani!" shouted Olga. A small wretched-looking woman was running wildly in the direction opposite to our own, followed by a hefty nurse in a white gown. Fleeing, she didn't see the barbed wire, her eyes blank, lost in the distance, her hair tousled. Her stunted body, childish almost, yet already shrunken, had discovered a new agility.

Vigevani had chosen to go into hospital because she was afraid of the work: her problem was her abnormal, underdeveloped body.

"The selection . . ." whispered Olga, shaken, "the selection Luciana told us about . . . She's trying to get away!" As she spoke, the head nurse's hand grabbed her victim's shoulder, Vigevani's eyes were wide with crazed fear.

The cover over the pit was located in the space between two huts, almost next to their doors. There was a nauseating smell. We pushed the cart closer.

"Come on, girls, three buckets each. Let's show we're as good as the men!" said Bianca Maria, and she climbed up onto a stool ahead of the others.

Another prisoner took a ladle with a long handle, dipped it into the pit and filled your bucket, then you lifted the bucket to face level and emptied it into the barrel on the cart. Three times. The work was humiliating, yet from it we discovered a new sense of dignity. The girls' movements were coordinated and graceful, the expression on their faces proud and severe.

I turned. On a wire near one of the huts some clothes had been hung out to dry. Red and turquoise—at last two brilliant patches of color in the middle of all that impossible gray?

With the cart filled to the brim, we set off to join the main road through the camp and then on toward the gate.

A young *Aufseherin* with coarse features and cap cocked to one side on crudely permed hair moved to the left to let the cart go by. She looked at us for a moment.

"*Scheisse!*" she said with a grimace of disgust for our foul existence.

4

The Presence of Death

Squatting on their bunks, the prisoners cut their bread into thin slices and covered them with margarine. They talked about the work, about the end of the war, about their homes far away.

"Where are the Italians?" asked the *bloccova*, coming toward the section where the eighty Italians who'd arrived with the last train slept.

"Who has Italian grandparents on both sides? Number?"

The talking stopped; the women leaned out over the edge of their bunks. The first arms stretched out as the *bloccova* checked the numbers tattooed on the skin and wrote them on a piece of paper; when

41

she had fifteen, she folded her paper and went off with a satisfied look.

Withdrawing into their bunks, the women clustered in groups, picking up their pieces of bread but without appetite.

They began to speculate. Obviously, nationality was being taken into account . . . Maybe this meant better treatment when it came to work? Some kind of guarantee? But then why had she taken only fifteen names?

The realization that it was absolutely impossible to make logical deductions offended that sense of the rational still active in the recently arrived prisoners. Nor for that matter had they reached the stage when, having substituted destiny for logic, they could get a feeling of satisfaction at being the sort of ball that will seek and immediately recover its inner equilibrium, whatever the whim of external circumstance.

"Tomorrow," the *bloccova* had said, "the numbers called out mustn't go to work but await further orders in the hut."

The same thing had been happening on the other side of the hut.

"*Que quiere de nosotras, niñas?*" said the Greek women whose numbers had been taken down.

The night passed, likewise the following morning. The other prisoners had left the hut to go to work, feeling a tinge of envy for those who wouldn't have to face the cold.

After a while we heard the heavy steps of the

Blockführer coming up the aisles between the bunks for his inspection. The whole room was full of his uniform and boots.

"Ah, ah, Italians," sneered the officer. *"Badoglio, Badoglio . . ."*

The mocking laugh echoed in the minds of these chosen prisoners. "What about nationality then?" they asked themselves over and over. "Nationality . . . what can it mean?"

In the afternoon the two groups of Italian and Greek women were taken to the hospital surgery.

The waiting room to the surgery was a small square space with two benches. In the corner opposite the door sat a young Polish girl, her complexion still fresh, her face round. A kerchief hid her shaved head. We sat next to her.

The joy of sitting in a normal position without having to cross or bend your legs! It was a long wait and the room was packed: the air got heavier and heavier.

The Polish girl spoke first: "Italians?" she asked, amazed, and looking at us added, *"So schöne Mädchen!"*

"You came on your own?" I asked her.

"No, with my family."

"Where are they now?"

She lifted her eyes, a finger pointing to the ceiling, and muttered: "All dead."

"And the camp for families?" asked Olga.

"Ach!" The Pole laughed. *"Das Familienlager ist das Krematorium. Alle vergast und verbrannt."*

She spoke flatly, her voice quite natural. I stared at her in disbelief, with hostility almost.

"Maybe at the beginning of the war, three, four years ago," we thought, "but not now, it's impossible." The Pole seemed to get some kind of pleasure from dashing our hopes, a sort of satisfaction from plunging us so brutally into the desperation that had once been her own.

After a long pause, as if following some habitual line of thought, the woman added; "... *und wir auch ... am Ende ... alle ins Krematorium.*" Her features didn't move, her expression didn't change.

—

The Greeks had gone in ahead. The checkup went on all morning—listening to your breathing, measurements, photographs ... There was no time for the Italians that first day or the second. Gradually, we realized we were being looked at in a different way by the other prisoners. When we went by, we heard, "I don't envy them, that's for sure; they're going to the Experiment Block. They keep them there to use as guinea pigs."

The news was confirmed by some Greeks who had already been in the camp for quite a few months. They told of appalling surgical operations, the removal of genital organs, mysterious injections with unknown effects repeated on several occasions, maybe in an attempt to produce sterility, abdomens disfigured by monstrous scars ...

Guinea pigs, human guinea pigs, material used by doctors for racial studies!

There Is a Place on Earth

Strangely, the Greeks telling the stories, who had all been in the camp a long time, were not upset. "Better this way, girls," they said, "better than dying. They'll treat you a bit better, and you won't have to go and work. You won't die!"

I was overcome by a wild desperation. My deepest, most intimate femininity was anguished and rebelled. I thought of my body brutally mutilated, its vitality hacked away, of being forced to surrender that most female function that nature had imposed to the monstrous violence these Germans in their hatred and scorn had coldly devised for us.

I felt Zilly's hand on my shoulder. The tears and sobs found an outlet.

"This body, this body, do you understand, it's not even mine anymore, it's my husband's, my daughters'. I want a child, another child!" Memories of early motherhood, its infinite, overwhelming sweetness, flooded back like a torture, a physical need. Oh, the unforgettable touch of the newly born child, still attached to her mother's body, but already independent, the joy of feeling her little mouth shape itself into a tiny sucker at my breast!

—

Where the news originated it was difficult to say. It came to Block 13 like the echo of some great upheaval. All the working parties were talking about it, the toilets were full of it, the story bounced back to us from the infirmary. "The English have landed in France." Everybody knew about it, everybody

45

was talking about it, everybody added their own details.

"Calais. The landing worked perfectly . . ."

"They've opened a third front . . ."

The whole camp was in a state of excitement for days. On meeting, prisoners would smile at each other; when they gathered in groups you heard muttered words of hope and vague plans. Those who preferred to be alone allowed the emotion and excitement to build up inside themselves.

As at the sudden collapse of a dam, the waters of memory rushed back toward the lost homeland. Voices from the "outside world" came flooding back. "Our men," the women repeated, "they always said: the landing will be the turning point. In two months it could all be over."

"My father," another said, "my father was more pessimistic, but he said, definitely inside August. And it's the end of April now . . ."

"You'll see. There will be other landings in different parts of Europe. There should be one in Greece . . ."

". . . and one in Trieste."

". . . then maybe one in the South of France."

Everybody translated the time needed for these operations into days and months, they calculated the number of German divisions, their chances of holding out.

"Girls," they said, "we'll be the last. No more trains will arrive. But even for us it's only a question of months, days. The war must end, soon, otherwise . . ."

There Is a Place on Earth

"Before the winter, otherwise we'll be dead too."
"For sure. All wars finish before the winter . . ."

—

Twilight gave things and faces a tone of gray melancholy. She put her hands on her lap and lowered her eyes. In the few days she had been in hospital she'd changed. Already thin, her naturally olive complexion was earth-colored now; her shifting gaze seemed to be trying to escape a haunting vision.

"Don't make me talk about it, girls, for the love of God," said Adriana in a whisper of a voice. "It was terrible . . ."

"Tell us. And the others? All of them?" the other prisoners asked anxiously.

"All of them."

"Even Carlotta's mother?" I lowered my voice so that Carlotta wouldn't hear. "And Vittoria? And Alma and Tea and . . ."

I stopped because I understood from her expression more than from any blunt answer that we couldn't hope to see them ever again now.

In the next bunk their places were empty—one, two, three . . . fourteen, fifteen. Those spaces screamed. Where one or two were missing, the remaining women would have preferred to be crushed together as they had been before, and that night they huddled close to each other and the spaces stayed empty.

"In the morning," Adriana began, "after admittance, when we went into the hospital wards, they

47

suddenly announced that a German doctor would be visiting. There was an SS man with him and the women doctors in the hospital. The new ones didn't suspect anything. But the older prisoners ... It was Doctor Mengele. He comes on purpose from Berlin for the selections ... The word 'selection' went from bed to bed. You knew what was going to happen from the horrified faces of the hospital doctors.

"Some people ran for the toilets, some tried to get out, but the door was locked. Some tried to hide under the bed. Hopeless. We filed by nude in front of him and he chose. He read the numbers on people's arms and wrote them down on a piece of paper. He was calm, indifferent ..."

"The women who were seriously ill, the terminal cases, or with contagious diseases, right?"

"You're joking! You think Alma or Vittoria were seriously ill? They had the flu because they didn't have enough clothes, and they were shivering with cold at the morning roll call, standing still from four till six outside in this godforsaken country ... It would be spring in Italy ... They'd only just arrived, they were flourishing, not like some of the skeletons you see here ..."

She spoke vehemently, then left a long pause, but nobody dared to interrupt her now.

"You remember Vigevani, that little woman? She tried to escape from the hospital. As if there was no barbed wire!"

"Shut up, Carlotta's coming," someone warned. "She mustn't know anything about it."

Later Adriana went on: "Carlotta's mother was

near my bed. She kept saying, 'I feel sorry for Carlotta, my poor girl!' We all had tears in our eyes.

"When the visit was over," Adriana said, "we didn't know which of us had been chosen. Those whose numbers had been written down or the others. The hospital block was like a mental ward. I was stunned, paralyzed. The woman next to me was sobbing. Somebody by my bed was screaming, wanted to throw herself on the floor like a maniac. People were beating their heads against the planks of the bed. A madhouse, I'm telling you. I couldn't think of anything. The next day they called the numbers . . . Four hundred out of four hundred and forty! Transportation to the *death block.*"

"The what?"

"It's a block where you wait for a few days before being gassed. I and a few others whose fevers had gone down were let out. Yesterday the Germans gave the women still in hospital white bread and a nutritious soup—a celebration!"

Right at that moment we heard the noise of trucks inside the camp. We had been forbidden to leave the huts for any reason whatsoever.

"The trucks, the trucks are coming to get them?"shouted Adriana.

Our faces turned suddenly white.

—

War and prison life have always generated new vocabulary. In the German camp in those years the word *organisieren,* "to organize," was appropriate.

"Organizing" meant swapping your bread for a

49

sweater, your margarine for a teaspoon. Anyone who snatches a piece of soap left by another prisoner in the shower or *Waschraum* is "organizing," and likewise the prisoner who hides a knife or a pair of scissors that have fallen out of the bed above and then swaps them for bread, or the prisoner who sneaks a couple of potatoes from a bin, or scrapes a few spoonfuls of stew from a *Kübel* . . .

There is no end to the ways prisoners organize, at everybody's expense. And anyone who doesn't organize is dead.

When you first get into the camp, you're incapable of organizing. You're shocked by the word every time you hear it, you hate it, and you ask yourself how it is that others have got things you haven't, how from having nothing they have been able to store away things. The novice prisoners know only one way of organizing: the least profitable—giving away their bread or margarine or salami rations for something they need even more than food that day.

When the Germans decide that after a certain day in April it's too warm to wear coats, all the coats are taken away.

It starts to rain, at night a cold wind rises, and at dawn the temperature has dropped. Who cares? The prisoners fall ill, they go into hospital, they die, or by some miracle they resist the tormenting cold. In the evening the women crowd round the block window: they swap a woolen garment for food. You miss your meal, one, two, three evenings in a row, consoling yourself with the faint warmth of the wool against your skin. But be careful of inspections: you might lose everything.

"No landing yet," said the most recent arrivals, French. "We would have known. We got here yesterday!"

"So when will the war end?" the other prisoners asked, losing heart.

"Oh, dans deux ou trois mois!" came back the mad, senseless hope of all Europe.

No landing, but there had been a selection. And it wouldn't be the last. The women saw work as their only chance of salvation. "Maybe as long as we can work, as long as the Germans can exploit our energy, they won't kill us . . ." and everybody was relieved when the news came that we were to be moved from Quarantine Camp A to Work Camp B.

Not everybody was moved at once. They took one work party at a time. The last ones left in the quarantine block were the women who pushed the cart, the *Scheisskommando*, and the mothers with children.

One day even the hard faces of the Ukrainians, triangular under the black kerchieves they wore across their foreheads, were running with tears. Grim and dark, with the jealousy of wild beasts, they hugged their children wrapped in bundles of rags to the their breasts. The Germans had given the order to separated mothers and children, those few, that is, who had been allowed into the camp together. The children were to be kept together in a separate hut, though who was going to look after them no one knew; how they were to be fed was a complete mystery. The women had to go off to the various jobs: the stones, the roads, the factories. Nobody had a right to live without working.

The children were taken from Block 13 too. Only the mother with the big dark eyes and withered breasts who was still breast-feeding was granted the privilege of keeping her children.

All the women, not just the mothers, sensed in the welling rebellion in their guts that something had been violently torn form the maternal instinct that lay at the very core of their being.

"It's better in Camp B!" said the prisoners who had already gone, as they passed us on their way to work.

"Bad news, girls!" one said one morning. "It was burning all last night. The flame was high!"

No point in asking what it was that had burned all night. It was that mystery, that anxiety, that nightmare that had become part of our natures. No one had seen it yet. We all felt the moment getting closer with fearful curiosity.

Finally, even the last prisoners left behind were moved to Camp B. Some went to the *Weberei*, the weaving party, some to the shoe party, the *Schuhkommando*.

Zilly, who was older than us, went to the *We-*

berei. Olga and I, huddling close together for fear of being split up, had the good luck of being sent to the *Schuhkommando* together with Dina and Ruth. The *Schuhkommando* had a reputation for being one of the best work parties.

The move to Camp B meant an end to the danger of being sent to the Experiment Block.

"They won't take us now," whispered Olga, and we looked each other in the eyes, a new bond tying us; fate had spared us both and was sending us off together to a common destiny.

5

Camp B

Camp B was identical to and symmetrical with Camp A. The same blackened, smoking, foul-smelling building housing the kitchens, with a huge heap of garbage and rotting vegetables outside; the same long hut with the showers; three rows of evenly spaced gray brick huts, and behind them, in the last row, the washrooms and the toilets.

The only difference was that where there had been the hospital in Camp A, here there were the slightly more comfortable green huts for the *bloccova* and *Aufseherinnen*. But the whole environment breathed the same grayness, the same desolation, the same humiliation: stones, muddy soil, barbed wire, clouds, and crows. Nevertheless, there was something different about the people: these ghosts with their ugly caps on their heads, crudely wrapped in rags hiding skinny limbs and sores, were heartened by a new boldness here. They showed no hesitation as they moved between the huts; when they went into washrooms and toilets, they weren't terrified they would be pushed away and clubbed. They didn't seem dazed and disoriented when they looked around. Their work had conferred dignity and rights, and the passage of time a deeper resignation.

People walked faster here; they were sly and sharp, yet at the same time more indifferent and dull.

The first sense of being better off came with the regaining of a certain independence (you could go to the washrooms and toilets on your own!), and with the introduction of something resembling organization in our lives: the fact that we worked meant there had to be a schedule for distributing bread and tea, and everybody was guaranteed an individual portion of soup.

The weaving party was housed in Block 25; in Block 27, exactly opposite Block 25, lived the *Schuhkommando*. All the Italians who had been together in the quarantine block were now split up into small groups housed in different blocks in Camp B, lost among the infinitely greater number of Poles, Slovaks, and Greeks, overwhelmed by foreigners with different national characters and sensibilities, women who didn't care for the Italians' open southern nature, so alien to brutality and hardship, so tenderly unprepared for camp life.

So we kept together, in pairs, like the valves of a clam, since to add to all the other dangers we had been through and prepared ourselves for, there was now the constant nightmare of becoming isolated, uncomprehended by the others, and hence their victims.

"Ach, du Franzuska," The Poles said scornfully, confusing the few Italians with the French; both groups felt a profound resentment for each other that had its distant roots in the different cultures and traditions that separate the northern slavic peoples from the Latin nations to the west.

When we arrived, Block 27 was still deserted. It was five in the afternoon and the work parties hadn't got back yet. The hut was dark inside. From a narrow window, at the bottom of the corridor, between the two lines of bunks, you could see the barbed-wire fence only twenty yards away, and beyond that another building, similar to the shower and kitchen buildings.

We sat on the edge of a bunk near the window waiting for the roll call. Two girls were leaning against the window frame and talking—one a Slovak *stubova* and the other a young Yugoslav.

"Ach," exclaimed the Slovak, moving her hand in a downward gesture, typical of the Germans but copied by the prisoners, "the end of the war . . . the end of the war." Once again the hope and enthusiasm that kept us tied to the outside world ran up against the wall of resignation, indifference, and pessimism raised by those who had been here longer.

"Dort sollen alle sterben . . . wir auch," and she turned her head, eyes coming to rest on the low building beyond the barbed wire.

"Why there?" I asked.

"Come on! Don't you know yet?" And she laughed. "The crematorium!"

We fell silent. It wasn't as we had imagined it. It wasn't a strange building; it didn't have a circular plan or anything recognizable as a crematorium. It was a simple brick building, like the huts but longer, with a tall chimney in the middle. Had it been surrounded by bricks left out to dry, it might have been a harmless kiln or a factory.

Perhaps there, that gray April dawn, our own mothers, our old folks, our children . . . The others went; I was sitting alone with Olga. The shadows in the block thickened and closed around our souls, bringing a sense that death was close by, present all around us, lying in wait.

"You know," I said softly, looking into the distance, "There was a small bunch of dry violets in mother's bag." They had been the first violets of that dazzling, wonderful Italian spring of 1944. "My little girl picked them for her granny, my husband's mother . . . they came with her all the way here, and through that door."

Giuliana Tedeschi

—

At dawn, after the roll call, the work parties lined up under the guidance of their *Aufseherinnen* along the large central road that crossed Camps A and B and led to the main gate.

Although it was late May now, the temperature in the night and early morning was biting cold: the tips of your fingers went purple, your arms and legs shivered and trembled all over and the women pressed their hands against their breasts. All the same, the clouds had gone from the sky, the flocks of crows flew high and far away, and along the edges of the hut roofs the very occasional twittering sparrow told of a spring already mature and fertile in lands farther south. The sun came up, an enormous ruddy disk; they were dawns that held a foreboding of blood.

At six o'clock the beating of a drum stirred numbed legs. At which the working parties swarmed off, heading out into the country in different directions: first was the "Canada," the luckiest and most highly regarded, hence its name. The women in the Canada wore gray-and-blue-striped uniforms with red kerchiefs on their heads. Their job was to look through and sort out the luggage abandoned by new arrivals when they climbed out of the trains that converged on Auschwitz from all over Europe. The Canada girls had a more florid, spruce look to them: even the worst off could always find a piece of chocolate, a candy, or a biscuit tucked away in some coat pocket or jacket, and in the evening, before coming back into the camp, they washed in the shower with real soap. Next came the "Underwear" party who again worked at sorting through luggage in the big cemetery at Birkenau, two miles away. Like the Canada, they had a uniform, this time with white kerchiefs.

After them came all the other working parties, dressed in rags: the Union party, who worked in the explosives factory, the *Schuhkommando*, the *Weberei*, who used the hair of the women deportees for thread, and all those who worked outside in the fields or on the roads, and who went under the name of the *Aussenkommando*.

A few yards from the main gate, on the right of the road, stood a hybrid orchestra of violins, cellos, a drum, an accordion, cymbals, and a double bass. They were conducted by a blond Russian woman who translated the urgency of rhythm and cadence into hysterical gestures. At fifty yards from the gate the working parties began their exit parade. Tired, emaciated limbs had to grow straight and proud, your aching feet bruised by ill-fitting, worn-out shoes had to march in line at a sure measured pace. Your stockings and underwear mustn't slip down, any bread or bowls had to disappear. Terrified, each of us were aware of having some forbidden object on us somewhere: a penknife or a pair of nail scissors in a pocket, a pullover against your skin, the things you really couldn't do without, bought by "organizing" your bread ration.

Each working party would stop for a few moments in front of the orchestra and mark time, while the musicians played a military march that German imperialism had made known the world over. Or they might play a cheerful aria from a Viennese operetta, the kind that walk-on characters in brightly colored clothes would come on stage to sing.

The German authorities in the camp would be lined up in front of the gate; to the left were the *Posten* with their wolfhounds tugging at the leash; to the right, behind a table, the *Blockführer* checked the numbers of the working parties, surrounded by officers and soldiers of the SS and women in uniform.

When the last beat of the drum had faded and you could no longer sense these heavy hawkish eyes on you, weighing up their prey, your chest would slacken and your breast heave with a sigh of relief, while your eye shifted to the ruddy disk of the rising sun and the freedom of the country.

The working parties walked across the fields toward a bare, desolate horizon; they went over the big arched bridge of the railway. Freedom passed by below in crowded trains: men and women returning to work from the demobilization centers. The prisoners looked down and their hearts were heavy: everything moved fast down there, everything was in motion—the trains, the doors opening and closing, the gestures, the looks exchanged; up above, everything was still, closed, monotonous. A

leap, an impossible leap onto the roof of a carriage
was all that separated us from freedom! The work
parties did not walk through the town: all we ever
saw of it was the thin church spire and a few sloping
roofs, from which we deduced neat, clean houses
with geraniums under the windows.

The country here had taken on a warlike face:
you walked past engineering workshops where the
men's parties worked, and turning the corner there
was the din of the Union factory. Another stretch of
green countryside and you reached the Canada
huts, with suitcases, baskets, blankets, and all kinds
of household goods piled outside.

To the left the country seemed to come to an end
in a group of buildings and huts. First there was the
large *Kommandantur* building with its clock, its
hands always at quarter to seven when we passed
in the morning; then the bakery, the laundry, and
the SS kitchens, and, opposite, the two ramshackle
huts of the *Schuhkommando*. We were away from
the camp but still not part of the real world. We
never met anyone but prisoners or German soldiers. The countryside wasn't natural and spontaneous: every inch of it had undergone some
transformation as a result of the war, was darkened
with the shadow of conquest and destruction, since
this stretch of land, as the Germans would proudly
vaunt, was not part of the Greater Reich but just
one of the many desolate areas of Poland where
people scattered in small villages suffered from the
grudging, unhealthy climate. Now it was swarming

with camps, never-ending lines of buildings; it had become an intricate, gigantic organism extending, save for brief intervals, for miles and miles, taking in salt mines and coal mines and malarial swamps.

The prisoners glimpsed just a small part of the fabric underpinning all this. Each in his or her camp was a pebble fallen into a well. But outside your camp you became a grain of sand in a desert.

6

Schuhkommando

The two huts of the *Schuhkommando*, one alongside the other, had been built with wooden beams, crudely put together and rotted by bad weather. In quite a few places the rain streamed in from the roof. The first hut was used as the workshop; it took its light from two rows of small glass-covered skylights in the roof and its air from the door. It was dark and damp on rainy days. The walls, the roof, the packing cases and sacks of shoes, the wet floor and the puddles that formed on the floor from water leaking through cracks in the roof, all gave off a stench of mold and rot. Along the walls groups of stools had been arranged around packing cases. In the middle of the hut a passageway ran from one end to the other. To the left of the entrance was a small room used by the working party's *Schreiberin*. The end of the hut, separated from the workshop by a wall made of boards, served as a storeroom.

In the second hut thousands upon thousands of dusty, decaying, moldy shoes were crammed together in the pitch dark, leaving only enough room to walk through along a central passageway.

The working party was made up of Greeks and Poles in a state of eternal rivalry with each other. The Greeks felt they should be in charge: they had built the huts three years before when this had still been nothing but empty country, bringing the planks from far away, loading the heavy sacks of shoes on their shoulders, working for months out in the open in the snow and frost. Only a few of the many who had started the job had survived, and every plank, every nail brought back memories of suffering and pain, often a story of death. Now, having risked their lives to build the place, they felt they had earned the right to work sitting down in a hut with a stove burning when it was cold outside, fed by the wooden soles of the clogs that would emerge from the heaps of shoes. Later, when the Germans increased the size of the working party, the Poles were brought in.

The women sat on stools from seven in the morning to six in the evening.

Every circle of workers had its own *Vorarbeiterin* who supervised the division of labor among the members of the group.

Apart from these groups, a team of girls, usually the youngest, was responsible for transporting the shoes in baskets and sacks from the second to the first hut and then distributing them to the groups of workers.

The shoes arrived in a constant stream through the door of the hut; the sacks stopped, swinging around each group until the shoes were emptied out in a cloud of dust to form a huge pile. This happened time after time throughout the day. It seemed there would never be an end to these mountains of shoes, and in the hours when one felt tired they weighed heavily on your spirits: from dead, empty objects they seemed to take on life again, intent on trampling on all our hopes and powers of resistance. Sometimes you had the feeling you were drowning in a sea of shoes. In the able, expert hands of the Greek women, sharp knives and heavy scissors flashed rapidly; hammers rose and fell fast and loud. Separated from their uppers, the leather soles fell in a constant stream into one case, while rubber soles went into another and the best pieces of leather taken from the uppers into a third.

The salvaged material would then be sent by freight train to Germany.

At first the four Italians who had joined the work party at the end of May and the few Frenchwomen who arrived soon after were each assigned to a group of experienced workers for training.

"Toma die Schuhe, italianika," said the Greek women. *"Mira, so . . ."* And in a flash they would be throwing the sole stripped from its shoe into the packing case. *"Abschneiden, verstehst du?"*

It was easy to communicate with the Greeks. They spoke Spanish mixed with Greek, they knew a few words of French, and they had picked up what German one needed to get by in the camp. Some of them even knew Italian or could understand it. They were almost all from Salonika, whence, two or three years before, the whole Jewish population had been deported en masse. They had clung to their peculiar way of speaking, that smack of cosmopolitanism typical of many Greek and Oriental cities. It was the youngest who had survived, almost all of them around twenty years old—faces with fine, regular features, straight noses, wavy hair. One sensed in their thin, sometimes immature, nervous bodies an extraordinary toughness. But in their expressions and movements they had hung on to something wild, something that had to do with their innermost natures. If they wept, they wept noisily with moans and groans. If they argued, they raised their voices in shrill cries, and the words went back and forth in torrents of Spanish and Greek with constantly ascending and descending parabolas; if they sang, they tended to choose Oriental-type dirges, monotonous and obsessive. "They're savages," said the French and

Italians condescendingly, though preferring them for their exuberant, southern nature to the tight-lipped, hostile Poles. They were amazingly fast and skillful when it came to working. They were capable of putting together a pair of sandals on the side, using rubber soles and bits of leather, or of repairing the heels and soles of a pair of shoes they'd found worth saving from among the thousands of useless ones; then when they got back to camp, they'd swap their work for bread, margarine, or soap. The Greeks all "organized" on a grand scale.

"Tiene hambre la muchacha," they would say among themselves, looking at us, and from among some rags under a basket one would pull out a thick slice of bread.

"Toma, italianika, Brot—essen," they said, and glanced quickly around. *"Nein, später."* They had realized that the *Aufseherin* had turned and was coming back down the aisle between the workers.

"Moco!" The word was shouted from one of the first groups. *"Moco, moco"* passed quickly in hurried whispers among the girls, and their hands began to fly, the soles fell one after another into the case, the scissors snapped, and heartbeats raced with the rhythm of the work.

"Moco, arbeiten, arbeiten," explained the girl with the bread.

Complete silence. A woman soldier was approaching from the door, maybe forty-five years old, wearing a gray woolen uniform, a military-style jacket with big pockets, leather boots that came up to her knees, and a cap cocked to the left.

Meanwhile in the second hut, a prudent girl had asked, *"En donde està la veija?"*

"A la primera barraca," they answered her, and the pairs of girls who brought the sacks of shoes to be taken apart and who took away the cases full of soles and uppers began to appear again at regular intervals.

The German walked by, looking at the heaps of shoes, checking the work, her hands in her pockets, strutting, then she was gone.

"Die Aufseherin," explained the Greeks and added, *"Gut."* Which meant she was zealous but not brutal. They called her Mirale—I don't know if it was a name or a nickname—and when she wasn't putting on her grim expression and saying *"Los, los, los!"* in her baritone voice, she looked as though she would have liked to laugh but had a candy in her mouth.

"Warum, 'Moco'?" I asked one of the Greeks. *"Was ist Moco!"*

"Moco ist Mirale, die Aufseherin, or rather *Frauseherin,"* said the Greeks, making a combination of *Frau* and *Aufseherin.*

"Ja, aber was ist Moco?"

The Greeks laughed. They didn't know how to explain in any of their languages, until one said, *"C'est la saleté du nez."*

"Ah, ah, Mocò." The French laughed. *"Travaillez mes enfants, bientôt va venir Mocò . . ."*

There Is a Place on Earth

The Greeks had retained a little humor. But woe betide the person who said anything to them about going home, or the defeat of the Germans, or the end of the war. They didn't want to hear such things, they didn't want to nurse hopes, they didn't care in the least who was winning or losing, how many miles a day the Russians were advancing, when the allied landing might be launched, what the consequences would be. They answered evasively or became gloomy. *"Ach, heute arbeiten und essen, morgen Krematorium."*

—

Our apprenticeship over, the *Schuhkommando*'s new recruits were brought together in two new work groups. The four Italians—Olga, Dina, Ruth, and myself—were overjoyed to find ourselves together again, working with the French.

Time passed; heaps of shoes followed upon heaps of shoes. There was no end to them. At night we dreamed of shoes; during the day we interpreted our dreams as signs of some new development. "Shoes in our dream, a journey on the horizon." The dust collected in our lungs; it stuck to our skin, causing irritating rashes. The scissors bent your fingers. The seats were hard and had no backrests, and with the long hours of work your back ached and your legs stiffened and shrunk in the cramped space between the packing cases.

Immersed in the muddled hum of the hut, I would find myself watching a sort of film in my mind; with extraordinary lucidity and no need for any effort to recall, a series of images passed before my inner eye—the corner of the street with the delicatessen next to where we lived, the facade of an attractive *palazzo* on the old circle of the Naviglio, our sunny house in the country . . .

What might have happened in the world meanwhile, no one knew. News that Hungary had surrendered got through the barbed wire, but everything was taking so long, too long for those who were losing a little hope every day. The Germans seemed to be the only ones in a hurry.

Since mid-May they had stepped up their arrests of Jews and political prisoners all over Europe to record levels.

Five, six, seven trains arrived in Auschwitz day and night from France, Belgium, Holland, and Italy. But most of the newcomers came from Hungary as a direct result of the country's collapse. The railway line had been extended with a new siding going from the station right inside the camp complex; it ended in the space between the men's and women's camps by the two buildings with the high chimney stacks. At dawn, when the work parties set out to work, they saw the trains rolling toward the camp and glimpsed tired sad eyes through the narrow windows. In front of the Canada huts, the piles of luggage had reached the roof and were still rising; blankets, quilts, and eiderdowns rose in great mounds, likewise saucepans, tins, and dishes of every kind.

There Is a Place on Earth

At sundown, far away across the country, beyond Birkenau, tall columns of smoke rose into the air that obsessed the knowing, anxious minds of the prisoners. At night the noise of wheels braking on rails, the confused clamor of the wagons being unloaded in the dark, the echoing of orders and the shouts of the Germans crept into our dreams, transformed them into terrible nightmares.

—

Leaving the *Schuhkommando* hut, the fresh air of the evening wrapped us in its merciful embrace. Numbed by eleven hours of immobility, our legs were desperate to be stretched; bent over rotting shoes all day, we straightened our shoulders with relief; our heads cleared; dry with heat and dust, our throats felt better for the contact with the air. There were two miles and more between ourselves and the camp: an hour's walk.

We moved in silence, letting the dusk and the countryside seep slowly into us: far away on the horizon was the fiery wheel of the sun, on both sides of the road green fields, above us the blue sky. Our nerves relaxed, our senses took their fill of air and light, our spirits sighed for liberty and envied the birds. The moment was sacred to us all. I would walk in silence beside Olga, cutting all the rest of the women out of my mind, sensing only her presence, though without looking at her.

That day at work a shoe had lain in my lap unfinished as I gazed into the distance.

"What are you thinking about?" Olga had asked. "A story—I'll tell you this evening."

On the road, at dusk, I began to tell her the story of a novella, Kuprin's *Seasickness*. Everything about us faded away. I imagined the small book in French translation on a shelf of my bookcase, saw my table laden with papers and pencils, smelled the smell of my study, rediscovered the emotion I'd felt upon reading the book for the first time. And my account was strangely detailed, full, extremely tense. I realized that Olga's spirit had become bound to my own and completely detached from the world around us. When I finished, she said, as if waking up, "Go on, please."

I too had been carried far away and didn't want to come back to the present.

"Listen to this *Lied* by Schubert," I said, and sang softly:

"Ich komme vom Gebirge her,
es dampft das Tal,
es braust das Meer,
es braust das Meer.
Ich wandle still, bin wenig froh,
und immer fragt der Seufzer:
wo? immer wo?
Die Sonne dünkt mich hier so kalt,
die Blüte welk, das Leben alt,
und was sie reden, leerer Schall;
ich bin ein Fremdling überall.
Wo bist du, wo bist du, mein geliebtes Land?

There Is a Place on Earth

gesucht, geahnt, und nie gekannt!
Das Land, das Land so hoffnungsgrün,
so hoffnungsgrün, das Land, wo meine Rosen blühn,
wo meine Freunde wandeln gehn,
wo meine Toten auferstehn,
das Land, das meine Sprache spricht,
o Land, wo bist du?"

> ("From the mountains I come,
> the steam rises from the valley,
> the ocean roars,
> the ocean roars.
> Full of sadness I wander in silence
> my sigh always asking
> where? always where?
> How cold the sun feels here
> the blossom fades, life seems to age,
> and all their talk seems empty noise;
> a stranger am I everywhere.
> Where are you, where are you, my beloved land?
> pursued, divined, yet never known!
> The land, the land so green with hope,
> so green with hope the land where my roses bloom,
> where my friends are wont to roam
> where my dead will rise to life again,
> the land that speaks my tongue,
> O land, where are you?")

My voice lifted with this last line and Olga squeezed my arm. It was our song; that land "green with hope" was our land, far away, dream-colored. All at once we started; two trucks raced by barely

73

a handbreadth away. They were carrying great piles of clothes bundled together haphazardly, and the sleeve of an overcoat swung out over the sideboard and filled with the rushing air, as if moved by an invisible arm in a gesture of protest. The notorious yellow star stood out starkly from a dark dress. At a bend in the road a baby jacket flew off the second truck.

In a flash I saw these clothes take on life, walk along streets all over the world: France, Belgium, Hungary, everywhere. Then from Germany the yellow star arrived. I saw men and women turn in suspicion and terror, get up from benches where "Jews can't sit," leave cafés and theaters where "Jews can't go." And though I had never worn it, I felt the weight of that star bearing down on me.

Now those clothes were empty husks, piled up and kicked around, but just as the smell of skin and sweat will cling, so these garments couldn't shake off the tragic humanity that had animated them until so recently.

In the distance the plume of smoke from two crematoriums rose high in the air.

Later, stretched out on her bunk before going to sleep, Olga told me, "Every evening you must tell me the story of a novel or sing me a song. For an hour at least we can live in a world where there are books, radios, phonographs."

The world where you are a Man or a Woman, not just a mere *Mensch*.

Along the main road through the camp the work parties were lined up silently near the hospital huts, waiting to go out to work. It was early June. A procession of women came out of one hut: shivering, they clutched dark woolen blankets from which protruded bare skeletal, unsteady legs. Each face shared the same waxy pallor; their ears seemed transparent, noses incredibly sharp. The women stumbled forward uncertainly. They were on their feet for the first time after their illnesses. Some were barefoot, others had their feet thrust carelessly into clogs or shoes that didn't match, all were naked under their blankets. Discharged from hospital, they headed for the showers: weaker, pushed to the limit, they thus returned to camp life.

"But that's Tea!" shouted one of the prisoners pointing to a thin figure in the group. And it was! Dear God, it was Tea. She heard our call and from far away raised a gaunt arm in salute. She might have been an apparition, a ghost. Yet it really was she, little Tea, alive before our very eyes, the Tea we had wept over as dead after the last selection. She had been so frail, a child almost, always trembling from the cold in her little sleeveless dress. But she had already developed a resigned detachment from life, a sense of surrender that had nothing childish about it at all.

That fatal morning of the selection two months ago, she had been one of those who had gone into the hospital. A sore throat and fever, the cold she'd caught at morning roll call in her light dress.

And we had waited for her return to the hut in

75

vain. She had lined up naked, not knowing what was going on, in front of the German doctors; then one of them had said to another, "What use is this shrimp?" And the other had answered, "Oh, let her go," and he had crossed out her number.

She appeared to us now as a sign that miracles could happen; we were filled with new hope.

"They've landed!" shouted an Italian from the other side of the road. "Cheer up, girls, we'll be going home soon!"

"Is it definite, Margherita?"

"Yes, yesterday, near Calais!" Olga and I embraced. "You know," I told her, "I don't want to believe it."

"*Que dijo, italianika?*" asked one of the Greeks.

"They've landed!" I answered.

"Who?" she asked, still indifferent.

"The English, of course!"

"And so, what's the difference? We're here?" commented the Greek, and she turned back to her own friends again.

"Think," Olga said to me, "if it's true, maybe in two or three months . . ."

"Right. Everybody has always said: the landing is the turning point. When the Germans have to fight on all fronts, they'll give up. They can't be so stupid as to go and get themselves invaded and destroyed. . . ."

We heard the echoing of drumbeats; the musicians struck up one of the regular marches. On the impenetrable faces of the SS lined up to watch us pass, we could find no confirmation of the news.

We walked in silence, each wrapped in her own thoughts. The country took on a new look, likewise the railway bridge and the station. Hopes remained unexpressed; it would be too risky to expose them.

That day at work everybody's hands moved feverishly, nonstop, galvanized by nervous excitement.

The great news spread through subterranean channels; it went from mouth to mouth, it grew, it took on details and convictions. "Have you heard? They've started the landing! This time it's true . . ."

Every sound died when the athletic figure of the *Arbeitsführer* accompanied by the *Aufseherin* suddenly appeared stark in the light of the hut door. Nerves tensed.

"Come on, what are you doing? Sleeping?" he shouted, walking by. And the *Aufseherin* in her masculine uniform smiled, as might any simpering flirt before a man; at once pleased with herself and adoring, she raised her eyes to the officer's face.

He walked in great strides as far as the end of the hut, then stopped, legs wide apart, arms folded. "Listen all of you!" We were all tense, but no one slowed down with their work. "You know what happens to the ones coming in on the trains."

The German woman gazed on with admiration: "What an adorably strong man," she was thinking. "All our men are like that!"

"Just get a load of Mirale's face," thought the prisoners, sneaking sidelong glances, "she's eating him with her eyes!"

"Well. If your work doesn't produce," the *Ar-*

beitsführer went on, "what we expect it to produce, you'll end up the same way—in the crematorium . . ."

The German woman's face darkened in suspicion. First she was hesitant, then came her undisguised assent in a big smile. "What a splendid idea!"

"Bang, bang, bang. *La putana vieja, la putana vieja,*" rapped out the Greeks' hammers.

"You know," Olga said, smiling, "I'm beginning to believe the English really have landed."

—

The *Schuhkommando* finished work later than the other parties, when most prisoners were already back in the blocks.

That evening, as we returned, a group of young women were lined up near the shower hut, all wearing the same expression of dazed embarrassment. Their clothes fell untidily about them and their heads were all shaved. But there was something in their abandonment and squalor that made us feel close to them.

"*Françaises?*" asked Olga, walking close to them. She was answered with a shout, her own name being called over and over in desperation and amazement. A girl ran out from the group and threw herself around Olga's neck, sobbing.

It was a moment for me to disappear, not to disturb that meeting, and I went back to the block alone, deeply moved. I had lain down on my bunk and I didn't hear her come in. I felt her weight lying on me, her arms looking for my neck, her tears wetting my face. I had never seen her cry before; she thought crying was a sign of weakness, or, rather, a prohibited outlet.

"Your sister?" I whispered, stroking her hair.

'Yes, the youngest. Oh! Vicky! Why did it have to be her?"

I didn't speak; I let her weep her grief. In a break in her story mixed with sobs, I risked the question: "And your father?"

"No, still in Italy." I heaved a sigh of relief. No crematorium then.

Gradually, Olga got ahold of herself and calmed down, and I discovered in my closest friend a maternal tenderness (it had been she who had brought up Vicky when her mother died) and a profoundly feminine side to her nature that hitherto, out of some strange feeling of shame, she had kept to herself.

"She's been here six weeks, she thinks," Olga went on, quieter now and drying her tears. "She recognized me from my voice. I wouldn't have recognized her among the others either." While she spoke, I was remembering how the girl had looked: rags down to her feet, haggard, the air of a frightened little animal. I'd been struck by her glasses, so big on that gaunt face. Eight months as a political prisoner in San Vittore prison in Milan, then deported as a Jew, and the poor little girl was only twenty.

79

From that evening on we referred to Vicky as *la petite*. Olga saved her bread ration for her, somehow managed to get hold of a piece of soap for her, dug out a strip of towel. In the morning when our party was lined up on the road waiting its turn to go to work, Olga sneaked off, slipped between the prisoners standing stiffly in front of the blocks for the roll call and bent down to hug her.

"Look," Dina told me, and squeezed my arm. "They look like two little birds. *La petite* with those glasses . . . all ready to run to meet her . . ." And Dina hung on to my arm from some instinctive need for tenderness. And I heard the Greeks asking: *"Ist sie die Schwester? Niña, mira; l'italianika* has found her sister!"

—

Nothing more has been heard about the war, absolutely nothing. It seems to have gotten bogged down far away. For the prisoners Germany's remaining strength means even harsher treatment.

When the *Posten* who escorts us to work is *une sale vache*, as the French say, she's isn't content to spend her time outside or in the SS rest house. She comes into the work hut followed by her dog, walks up and down, and starts to look at the women bent over the shoes.

Other than watching us, she has no way of passing the long morning hours, so she immediately notices when a girl talks to her neighbor or when she holds a shoe for a moment without taking it apart.

There Is a Place on Earth

"Komm, komm her!" There is an ironically inviting tone to her voice that sends shivers down everybody's spine. The unlucky girl is a Greek, arguing with her neighbor over possession of the scissors.

She gets up and goes to kneel down in the corner the *Posten* is pointing to.

"Nimm die Ziegel," says the German, *"zwei Ziegel. Hände hoch!"* With an effort the woman manages to lift her arms: two bricks are heavy to hold, arms outstretched above your head. When her arms get tired, they bend. The *Posten* sets the dog on her: *"Hoch! Hoch!"*

From where they're working the other prisoners raise their eyes from time to time. They suffer, they weep, humiliation weighs down on them like the weight of those bricks.

We work angrily. The soles are cut away violently, thrown scornfully into the box. We sense the minutes passing, and as a result time seems to stand still. The girl's arms start to tremble from the effort, her knees tortured by the rough floor, her legs have gone stiff.

How long has it been? An eternity for us. The *Posten* still won't put an end to this torment. And the girl summons all her strength; she holds on and on. Her forehead is beaded with sweat. In her terrible physical tension we sense all that wild, indomitable primitive strength that is part of the Greek character. *"Les grecques sont des sauvages,"* say the French.

But all at once her body doubles up, the bricks

81

fall, the woman is shaken by sobs, almost convulsions. It's not crying though. Her companions try to get her up, but she can't stand, her legs won't hold her. The others suppress a cry of terror and desperation.

Finally, the *Posten* remembers her: she is allowed to hobble back to her place.

Encouraged by these examples, even Mirale, our *Aufseherin* is getting used to the idea. The soles aren't properly cleaned, are they? The work hasn't been done carefully enough, has it? Well then, after they've eaten, the group leaders will have to do some "sports." Legs bent, the girls have to jump about the hut, do hundreds of push-ups . . . until the color drains out of them, they're exhausted, they start to retch. And if someone is guilty of sneaking off to the toilet, Mirale will keep the bathroom door shut for hours at a time, or at lunchtime she makes the whole party kneel down, without eating, in front of the closed drums of soup.

7

Punishment

Shoved violently out of the block, I fell to my knees on the bare earth. Thinner than ever, in the white nightshirt that left arms and neck exposed, my curly hair cut short, I looked like an adolescent. Around me was the vastness of the night: I buried myself in it, I took refuge in it. The starry sky was close, it was a friend. So cold and so foreign by day when it was almost always covered by big stormclouds, tonight that Polish sky had something mysterious and familiar about it, something of the sky of my home country far away. With joy I recognized the Great Bear, as if it were an old family friend, then the polestar, Venus with its three stars in line, all the same.

At that hour of the night the camp looked sinister, with its interminable rows of dark silent blocks, the barbed-wire boundary fence lit by powerful lamps all around, and the ghostly white path of the search-light ruthlessly coming on and off as it hunted down your humiliated individuality in the general misery. Inside the huts, huddled bodies vainly sought some rest after the daily toils, some respite from desperation. Everybody's sleep was disturbed, populated by ghosts; among the frequent cries and groans, the word "mama" could be heard coming like some distressed plea from the lips of the young sleepers.

In a silence and darkness deprived of the relaxation that night should bring, the stars seemed to belong to a different world, where our infinite misery was unknown. And in the abandon of the sleeping camp you saw that misery more clearly and sharply than during the gigantic struggle for existence that went on in the light of day.

I had violent pains in one wrist and down one side where the *bloccova*'s club had beat me just a few minutes ago to remind me not to break the *Lagerruhe,* the strict silence that must be kept after eight in the evening. There would have been no point in trying to explain that I hadn't slept for three nights, that I was literally suffocating, crammed and crushed between eight other prisoners, that a Belgian was stealing my place, that . . .

There Is a Place on Earth

The ground was hard, and clods and pebbles pressed into my flesh. I clutched my arms to my breasts and shivered in that May night, frosty as an Italian night in February. Never before had I had such a strong feeling of being a grain of sand lost in the infinity of the universe. I was seized by dismay and desperation. In front of me the block windows reflected the light of a fire, and the same red flame flickered across a hundred other windows. The whole camp seemed to be on fire. That flame . . . I tried to find some way not to see it but couldn't. High up, over the chimney of the crematorium, commanding the scene, it had reddened a corner of the sky. It burned night and day.

I heard the confused sounds of people who had got off the train and were heading, unawares, to the doors of the mysterious building. I didn't dare turn around, that glow paralyzed me, and in my state of spiritual prostration an overwhelming desperation took hold of me. Something appalling had happened before my eyes, something which so far I had sought at all costs to avoid and which tormented me far more than the pain in my wrist and knees. I had been shaken to the core, my human dignity had been violated, violated by an abject being who knew nothing of me or the world. I threw myself facedown on the ground and wept and suffered terribly at the thought that I had a husband and children. I wanted to be alone, to be the only one who need think about my destiny.

From a lookout post came the sound of an accordion accompanied by a grating male voice: the guard *Posten*, who watched over all this misery in the constant presence of that flame, had found a way to pass the time and relieve the boredom of his watch.

Two delicate hands laid a smock on my shoulders, and a voice I didn't know muttered something. I recognized her in the glow from the flame: A Frenchwoman, quite old, who worked in the *Schuhkommando*, one of those dull creatures, without life or intelligence, who in normal circumstances barely manage to get by, and who in the camps seemed mad and moronic.

I threw my arms around the neck of this companion in punishment, while to console me she whispered; *"Ça va finir, mon petit, ça va finir; bientôt!"*

8

Sundays in the Camp

It was still pitch dark when the siren that sounded reveille went off in the camp. We looked with surprise through the narrow hut windows at the starry sky, then got up, mute and bad-tempered.

Sunday was the long-awaited day dedicated to patching up clothes that were falling to pieces or washing your only pair of underwear; but above all it was the day when you could sleep an extra hour and wake up without being herded out into the dark, when you would go out of the hut to lift your face to the mother-of-pearl sky of dawn!

But some time ago now the Germans had decided

to deprive us of the one distinction between the seven days of the week by abolishing Sunday rest. After the roll call all the work parties were taken off to do a special job: we were to pick up the bricks that littered the railway embankment between the women's camp and the men's camp, and carry them from one part of the complex to another.

Along the track, panting and asthmatic, a long train gave a last whistle like a tragic lament: a premonitory signal, but the people in the wagons took no notice. Only the camp prisoners were shaken, day and night, by the lacerating cry.

The work parties marched in rows of five to the railway line. Slithering haphazard down the embankment where their clogs wouldn't grip, the women fell on top of one another. They got to their feet with an effort under the weight of four bricks and climbed back up the steep slope. The Germans kept their dogs at the prisoners' ribs and followed their stumbling steps with angry snarls: *"Los, weiter, schnell!"*

Meanwhile, men, women, and children of every age, filthy and tattered, climbed out of the wagons, disheveled after their interminable journey in the cattle trucks. An enormous tiredness, the waiting for and resignation to an inescapable destiny was stamped on each face, and yet they showed no sign of being aware how imminent and tragic the end was. The SS officers and soldiers made their selection, separated them into two groups, and sent one off to the right and one to the left: to the right the old, the weak, the women with children in their arms or held by the hand; to the left the men and young women who would provide fresh energy for useless tasks.

The prisoners had to go very close to the train, barely two or three yards away. The new arrivals watched, distracted and inexpressive. "In a few hours," they thought, "once we're behind the wire, we'll be like you: beasts of burden, persecuted and loathed." The men and women were still so human, so miserably human, that the prisoners could barely contain their emotion and lowered their faces: at least we wouldn't betray our knowledge of the tragedy that awaited them!

A Hungarian girl fell to the ground, writhing, her mouth in the earth. She had left her father behind in Hungary, in a rest home, and now her anxious gaze had found him in the line to the right, with the old people, hunched and dazed, setting off along the road.

We were morally destroyed, physically exhausted; the awareness of our impotence humiliated us, the instinct to rebel choked us. Sweat streaked burning faces under suffocating kerchiefs; clothes took on an even more wretched look, soiled by the earth and the red dust of the bricks.

Among the people to the right, an old woman, unkempt and tattered, walked forward with a baby asleep in her arms. A tiny hand swung loose against her body as the child's head lay in trustful sleep against his grandmother's shoulder. My little girl, I held you again then, just as I'd held you that last night when you went to sleep on my breast after a long tantrum. The last night at home: that tantrum had cost a small, but first, argument with my husband. And it would have to be the last.

A sob rose in my throat, but I had learned to bite my lips and stop the tears under my lids.

The end of the road was dominated by the low building with the high central smokestack. The flame and a plume of smoke rose from the top. The people to the right had reached it now. They were waiting to go in. They crowded around. They tried to get ahead in the queue. Tired from their journey, they all imagined they were about to have a refreshing shower.

Meanwhile the whole camp was gradually pervaded by a smell that only we old hands could recognize, the smell that haunted our nostrils, that impregnated our clothing, a smell we tried in vain to escape by hiding away inside our bunks, that destroyed any hope of return, of seeing our countries and children again—the smell of burning human flesh.

Humanity had lost its voice: the women with the bricks were mute; the people on the right walked silently along the road to the crematorium. But in a separate corner of the camp the orchestra had been set up. The rhythmic notes of jolly marches filled that great silence and galvanized the most tense, worn nerves.

"Madness!" I said to myself. "This is where madness begins!" A whirl of images, of faces revolved kaleidoscopically and incessantly in my brain, pictures etched themselves confusedly without selection or order.

"Du, komm her!" An arm suddenly pulled me out of line. I had to help take some *Kübel* with soup and potatoes from the kitchen to another camp.

I was tottering; I didn't know how I could lift the huge weight of the drums. I realized then that I hadn't eaten anything since the evening before and it was nearly noon now.

I don't know how it happened; I still wonder today: some animal instinct prompted me to throw myself on the drum with the potatoes. Taking advantage of the confusion, I filled my pockets, I ate in bites without taking off the peel. I felt only one thing inside, a dark sensation that grew and grew, the inextinguishable need to live, despite the SS, the camp, the crematorium.

When the job was done, I got back to our block exhausted and lay facedown on my bed without speaking, my head on my arm. Olga was beside me.

"Tell me a story," she said softly.

"Yes . . . a story," I said. "The story of here and now. *A true story.*"

———

"Oh no!" said Bianca. "The hell with Sunday *Läusekontrolle* [lice inspection] always coming at dinnertime!" Glancing at the steaming mess tins, she left the hospital in her white doctor's gown and set off toward the work camp. She went through the gate between the camps and crossed the whole of Camp B as far as the furthest huts. Beyond the perimeter, inside the crematorium fence, smoke was rising from a shallow round pit.

"They look like pots, those round things," Bianca thought to herself and, intrigued, went up to the barbed wire. But all at once she turned, pale, swaying on her feet, and ran and ran for as long as she could, only remembering *Läusekontrolle* when she was already far away and out of breath.

She told nobody what she had seen, that in the pit, all lying next to each other, a host of human heads were roasting slowly like chestnuts on the grate.

—

Fifty women were rounded up for a special job that Sunday. The column set off toward the exit followed by an armed *Posten*. At the checkpoint they stopped to be counted, then went through the gate. But they didn't turn left as they usually would to go to the main gate in the boundary fence and the road that led out of camp.

Instead, to everybody's surprise, they turned up the big dusty avenue that separated the women's camp from the men's. On both sides barbed-wire fences marked the end of rows of identical huts.

Having left Camp B, the women realized for the first time that Camps A and B were not the only ones. As far as the eye could see, the vast plain was seething with camps; and in the spectral figures toiling everywhere they saw their own martyrdom multiplied a thousand times.

To the right ran the railway line, the most recent siding that the Germans had built from the station to the camp.

A faint sense of unease began to take hold of them: this squalid road had something funereal about it. It was here that the transport wagons stopped, that their human cargo herded together from all over Europe was unloaded. It was here that the men, women, and children went through the first sorting process that declared them suitable for torture or for death.

At the end of the road, two buildings, one immediately recognizable because it was located inside the women's camp, the other symmetrical and inside the men's camp, formed a dismal backdrop. Beyond those buildings the road became a path again, striking out across a copse of birch trees.

For the prisoners approaching there was nothing unknown or mysterious about this. They knew that those long buildings with the slim smokestacks were two crematoriums. They had seen the tops of them so many times "Is it burning? Can you see the flame? Is there smoke?"

They walked slowly, and it seemed that from the bottom up the smokestacks grew enormous, were advancing on them, wanted to stretch out and snatch their prey.

"Krematorium . . . crematorio . . . crématoire,"

the women began to mutter: everybody whispered the word, and everybody understood it in every language. They couldn't take their eyes off the chimney. The message passed from one to the next and the tension grew. Nightmares were becoming reality. "In rows of five—*pente kai pente*—*zu fünf nach Krematorium . . .* " A Polish girl was the first to weep. She thought of friends who had been selected at roll call, in the showers, in the hospital, and had never come back to the huts. The Greeks had wide, dilated eyes, holding their breath. The agitation of the most recent prisoners became desperation in those who, having been in the camp for years, had by sheer luck survived a hundred encounters with death.

The women walked by the two crematoriums, turned right, and took the path through the birches, a small oasis. The elegant trees sketched arabesques across the sky with their rustling foliage. Once they must have covered the whole area now devastated by the construction of camps. None of the women was aware of the wood, of the birds singing, of the rustling leaves, the whiteness of the bark, the blue of the sky. The path led toward Birkenau: behind the wood, hidden by the trees, rose the red-brick mass of another crematorium, the biggest.

The women went in through the big door and stood in the hall. Waiting for them were fifty baby carriages. The German soldiers ordered each of them to take a baby carriage and push it, in rows of five, for two miles, to the warehouse where the loot brought with each train would be collected and sorted.

The nervous tension drained away, yet each face was stamped with a grimace of pain. The strange procession moved forward: the mothers who had left children behind rested their hands on the push bars, instinctively feeling for the most natural position, promptly lifting the front wheels whenever they came to a bump. They saw gardens, avenues, rosy infants asleep in their carriages under vaporous pink and pale blue covers. The women who had lost children in the crematorium felt a physical longing to have a child at their breast, while seeing nothing but a long plume of smoke that drifted away to infinity. Those who hadn't had children pushed their carriages along clumsily and thought they would never have any, and thanked God. And all the empty baby carriages screeched, bounced, and banged into each other with the tired and desolate air of persecuted exiles.

9

Thirst

The Polish summer arrived—scorching days, damp, cold nights. In the immobility and monotony of camp life the passing of time was apparent only in the scars it left on our bodies and minds. Olga was gloomier and less expansive as she worked; Dina's shoulders hunched and fever flushed her cheeks; I wept over baby shoes; and Jacqueline, the French-woman in our group, grotesque face tipped back, dreamed of Bandol on the Var coast, of a garden sloping down to the seas, of pistachio ices and an elaborate hairdo on her head, where at the moment there was nothing but a couple of inches of prickly, unkempt shag.

There Is a Place on Earth

The sharpened faces, dull, lost eyes, and exhausted bodies of your friends were your condition too. Sometimes tongue, throat, and palate would ache with the onset of vitamin deficiency and you couldn't even swallow a crumb of bread.

Much of the unseasoned, often unsalted turnip slop would be left uneaten in our bowls. In the last few months the potatoes, barley, and margarine they used to put in it had disappeared, while the dose of bromide had been increased, giving the food a disgusting, bitter taste.

As if there were any need for bromide! Those bodies that left their broth behind in the bowls at lunch break, huddling up on two stools or on a heap of shoes on the ground to snatch a moment's sleep despite the surrounding din, had neither vitality nor sex. Having lost their menstruations as a result of malnutrition and shock, the women no longer felt they were women. Men were husbands, brothers, companions in misfortune; there was the distressing thought of their fate and their suffering; but after a month in the camp no one spoke of a man as a lover anymore. "When we get back," the Italians and French would say—and they would add, "if we get back"—"when we get back, we shall be different; people who haven't been through this hell won't understand us."

Something had changed deep inside us. Sensitivity had been numbed, the capacity to be moved had gone, we had developed the habit of reducing life to a few bare essentials and there arose the need to hate and curse. We thought if ever we returned, this transformation would condemn us to solitude and incomprehension.

Its wooden walls scorched by the sun, the hut became suffocating. The air coming in through the door wasn't enough to refresh the women sitting on their stools, bent over the shoes, faces running with sweat. The back of the mouth and all the mucous areas from throat to windpipe felt like cork. The heat and parched atmosphere produced by the dust condemned us to inhuman torments of thirst. But the only water was in the SS kitchens, where the hut workers were allowed to draw only two pails a day.

In the worst hours of the afternoon we were in such a state of nervous tension, our trembling hands could barely hold scissors and knife. Our foreheads burned and our eyes were bright with fever.

At last the water came, was poured from the pails into red-enameled bowls and distributed to the prisoners: one bowl for every group, not more than two mouthfuls per person. Our hands idle in our laps, we couldn't take our feverish eyes away from the red bowl as it passed from mouth to mouth, watching the throat of a neighbor lift twice in two long mouthfuls, as if the neck were transparent and we were seeing a few drops of water poured away into sand.

If somebody's lips should hang onto the rim of the bowl a moment longer, their throat rise and fall a third time, the others would all yell out, feeling cheated. Once back in camp, who wouldn't dash to the washrooms, thrust their head under a jet of bitter, rusty water to at last satiate the furious thirst that was driving us crazy? Who took any notice of the signs DON'T DRINK. Who wasn't convinced that it was better to die of typhoid than of thirst?

When you came out of the *Schuhkommando* hut at sundown, your head was heavy and on fire; your ears buzzed. On the opposite pavement, right near our workshop, the cases of soda and mineral water for the SS mess rooms rose up in great stacks. But if, in a moment of mad, foolish daring, a hand of ours were to flash out and grab one, eyes darting around wild and afraid, two or three Greeks would leap on you as if you'd touched a red-hot iron.

"*No tomar esto, italianika!*" They tore the bottle from your hand, a dark madness in their determination.

"Two years ago," Buena explained, "coming out of work on a stifling day like this, someone hid a bottle under their dress. 'Go on, go on, you take some too!' said the *Posten* to the others, laughing. We all came back to the camp with bottles hidden in our clothes. At the gate our party was stopped for an inspection. It was the *Posten*, you understand; the *Posten* had telephoned to warn the guards! We knelt down in front of the block and waited to see how it would end. 'Take your clothes off!' said the *Blockführer*. Trembling, stunned, each of us let her clothes drop to her feet, even our slips. '*Und jetzt, marsch, nach Krematorium! Eins, zwei, drei, links; eins, zwei, drei, links . . .*' Naked. At the end of the

99

road, 'Halt': this time they'd let us off, we could go back to our block!" And Buena sighed.

Apart from the heat, the summer had brought another profound change. For months and years as the war progressed through its various phases, the prisoners had waited for the moment when it would remember them; but thousands of men and women had died waiting and the survivors had got used to the stalemate. Then all of a sudden our ears picked up the friendly drone of airplanes: small squadrons of Russian planes began to fly over the camp day and night, to the surprise and consternation of the Germans. When the raids grew more frequent and a few bombs fell near the station, when the clock on the *Kommandantur* stopped and all its windows were shattered by the explosion, the Germans sounded sirens and set up smokescreens around the factories and mechanics' workshops.

Finally one day we heard dull thudding echoes in the distance; isolated at first, then a prolonged indistinct rumble.

"They're not bombs," said the women, whose ears were getting attuned to explosions.

"They're not the thuds of tree trunks being loaded on wagons; they're farther away," they said, listening hard over the din of their hammers. "The Russian artillery must be getting near Cracow."

10

The Specter of the Camp

First you only know its name. It's the specter of the camp who seizes us prisoners the moment our strength fails. You grab hold of the bowl with the tea to quench your thirst and a friend warns, "For God's sake, don't drink too much. Heaven only knows what herbs it's made of: it'll give you diarrhea!"

You look at the yellowish turnips in the soup, pieces usually fed to pigs and cows, and you ask, "Will it give me diarrhea?"

Then one day at roll call, stiff with cold, a woman twists around, goes pale, feels she's going to faint.

She wants to run, but roll call is sacred, no one has the right to move. She squeezes her legs together and beads of cold sweat stand out on her forehead; she's being crushed under a great weight, but she can't just lie down on the ground. And so the inevitable happens. She's no longer human; she feels ashamed and she groans, exhausted. From now on she can get no peace: she has washed her underpants, but she doesn't know where to dry them and she has no others to put on. Then she fears it could happen again any moment. She runs to the toilet: she finds all the places taken. She begs: "Quick, please, I've got diarrhea!"

The others look at her with unsympathetic eyes. "Me too. I can't get up."

She doesn't know what to eat. If she's lucky, she manages to toast herself a few slices of bread over the stove or to swap half her ration for a raw potato. This is the medicine. But she has to work just the same. Every day she gets yellower, weaker; the parching thirst devours her.

When she can't stay on her feet anymore, she goes to the hospital. She doesn't eat, her bread ration accumulates, and she just drinks. Then the fever comes, she's delirious: "Mama, it wasn't me! It wasn't me dirtied the mattress!" The next day the nurse bangs on the side of the bunk to distribute the bread. No response: the woman lies cold and contorted, her bottle next to her inert body.

"Tery's dead. Diarrhea!" The word gets around;

the message is passed on as one work party encounters another.

Many have already died, in the April selection or from some illness or other in hospital: typhoid, scarlet fever, influenza . . . Watching them go in, the other prisoners shake their heads and tremble. Only a few come back, transfigured, skeletons; of the others nothing more is heard, they won't walk this earth again.

"My sister," tells Thérèse, "had a pain in her legs; she couldn't handle the work. She went into hospital, two weeks after getting here. One day I get back from work and go to see her. 'Your sister,' the nurse tells me, 'was taken away in the selection!' What was I supposed to do? I wept, I didn't eat for two, three days. I would wake up with a start in the night. But I didn't die. I want to live, I do! I want to go back to France!"

I no longer dash to the weaving hut of a morning to see Zilly for a moment. I don't have to say good night to her anymore.

"They've changed camps; they've been switched to easier work," say the surviving women to brothers, sisters, husbands asking for news; or they write their compassionate lie on a scrap of paper with a stub of pencil. The note goes from hand to hand; it brings a little relief, or at least it doesn't increase distress. "In any event," we all think, "sooner or later we'll be dead too, in the hospital or the crematorium . . ."

The survivors meet in the toilets or the washrooms; the sun has given your gaunt, tanned faces a metallic hardness; those who work outside have enormous blisters on their legs; sometimes a clubbing will have left big purple bruises on the skin; vitamin deficiency has covered your limbs with horrible sores; your hair has been shaved time and again; your leanness has dug hollows in arms and legs. You can barely recognize each other.

And for each friend you have a double image; how they look now, how they were before.

11

Ruth's Story

"Is your husband here too, Ruth?" asked Jacqueline. And she added, "Who's got the scissors?"

Ruth didn't answer, but her hammer blows on the sole of the shoe became more violent. Olga threw a shoe at Jacqueline's legs to shut her up; I raised my eyebrows in warning. There followed a pause heavy with the noise of hammers and the deafening clamor of the hut. Jacqueline bent forward to pick up her knife, and I whispered in her ear, "Shot by the Germans, tell you about it this evening."

Again Ruth's hammering drew my attention. She was busy putting heels on a matching pair of shoes that had appeared miraculously from the heap.

Dina was keeping watch, and at every alarm Ruth hid the good pair and picked up a moldy shoe to take to pieces.

"You work like a real shoe mender," I said with admiration.

"I was a shoe mender, among other things. I learned from my husband in Nice. We'd escaped there as refugees, shortly after we got married. We still had a few jewels and a little money, but it wasn't enough to last long, and even selling those and my mother's fur coat, we would have to find something else soon. So my husband remembered that when he'd been a soldier in Africa he'd learned how to make shoes. He bought the tools. He worked and laughed. I kept him company and watched. That's how I learned. Thank God! It means I can do a little 'organizing' for Dina now; she's not eating anything. I don't know what I'd do if I didn't have her to care for. What reason would I have for living? Look at her: she's waxy, transparent."

Dina said, "Watch out, Ruth!" and at the same time the Greeks began their warning cry of *"Moco!"* Ruth hid the shoes in time. Mirale went by. The talking stopped, everybody set to work, doubling their speed: the hammer blows vied with the snipping of the scissors. Mirale took a look to see how many shoes were in the case and out of habit hissed, *"Los, los!"*

When she'd left the hut, everybody relaxed.

"Where were you, Ruth, before coming to Italy?"

I asked her. Ruth began to nail on the second heel.

"We escaped from Germany to France—Mom, Dad, and me. I was ten. We got by as best we could. We still had a bit of money and Dad did some casual work. Then the really bad times came around; you had to hide. One day Dad and Mom were arrested and deported. And now I know where they came . . ." Her expression clouded over.

"And you?"

"I was put in a children's camp in France. There was no food. Six months later we were all skinny, yellow, with huge stomachs! Then I managed to escape. For six months I hid in peasants' farms, looking after the animals. Then I went to Nice. That was where I met my husband, a refugee from Austria."

After a few minutes Ruth said, simply, "We loved each other a lot. Our characters complemented each other: I'm sad and moody, and he was always happy and optimistic. We left France and went to Italy, out in the country with the partisans—"

"*Mittagholen!*" shouted the voice of the *Vorarbeiterin*. It was time for soup.

"Ruth, have you finished the shoes?" asked Dina.

That evening, lying beside Jacqueline on our straw mattress, I began to tell her Ruth's story.

"I'd already been in prison about a week, the Nuove prison in Turin. One morning we were in the tiny yard, where they'd send five or six of you for an hour to get a breath of fresh air, when a new prisoner was pushed in. She was wearing a pair of blue trousers, the kind people wear in the mountains, a torn flannel blouse and a dirty, crumpled raincoat. She had a big pair of hobnail boots. There was still a childish softness about her face, except that the mouth had a bitter expression. Her eyes were vacant, utterly distant from reality. She leaned on a wall with an expression of indifference.

" 'Why are you wearing boots?' the nun watching over us asked, looking with obvious disapproval at her men's clothes.

" 'They picked me up in the mountains,' the girl excused herself, 'and I've got nothing to change into.'

" 'Have you eaten?' a fat old woman asked, one of those put in prison for being active socialists.

" 'No.'

" 'Since when?'

" 'Three days. We ate snow.'

" 'Where were you?' We had all gathered around her.

" 'They betrayed us . . . The cowards! The Germans came for us, from every side, lots of them, armed. They surrounded the mountain . . .'

" 'Where?'

" 'Casteldelfino, above Cuneo. We fought to the last. Three days and three nights fighting without a break, in the snow, without eating. I barely had time to load the rifles and throw the grenades.' She touched her right arm. 'My muscles are still aching. But in the end they got us,' she said wearily. 'Three partisan officers, me, and my husband.' I raised my eyes to her face in surprise; she was so young, still a little girl, but with a wedding ring on her finger. 'They interrogated us all night. They wanted other names. Then a German said, "Shot her too; we've got no use for these filthy Jews." And instead they took away the men. My husband yelled, "Ruth! Ruth!" I heard four shots, then nothing. In the morning they put me on the train and brought me here. Now I'll be deported. I don't care about anything anymore.' "

"Terrible," Jacqueline said.

"That's not all. You know Ruth is German," I went on, "well, six years ago, when she was twelve . . ."

12

Word from Home

"Hey, girls, Olga . . . Giuliana!" A face with bright gray eyes was looking in through the window of the block.

"How's it going, Bianca Maria?" I asked, running to meet her.

"I've got a parcel from home and a letter from my husband!" The tears ran silently down her cheeks; she bent her head and was shaken by sobs.

"Bianca Maria, what's wrong? Come on, cheer up, you should be happy. Getting a letter! But that's fantastic, and what does it say? How did he send it and how did you get it?" We fired questions at her.

"Through Lucia, that girl from my village who works in the *Aussenkommando*. The Germans deported her as a hostage because her brother went to join the partisans in the mountains. One day I said to her, 'Lucia, you write home once a month, right? They let you Aryans write, but we can't. Do me a favor, write 'Bianca Maria is well and sends her greetings to the pharmacist in Piazza Rendenzione.' And now she just got a letter addressed to 'Cara Lucia,' but in fact it's for me." And again she burst into tears. "It says . . . it says . . . that my little boy is well, he's in the country and he always asks after his mama, and . . . he says that ever since they arrested me I've always been in his thoughts and always am . . . he hopes that I won't have to suffer too much . . . he's sure he'll see me again soon."

"Great, so why are you crying?" I began to reproach her. "Now you've got some good news, you cry and lose your strength . . ."

"You know how it is," she said, trying to cheer up. "Your nerves can hold out just so long, then you reach a point when you can't handle it anymore. And when I saw his writing . . . you know . . . Oh, I can't stand it, I can't, I'll never go back . . ."

Olga tried to joke, to change the subject.

"Aren't you even going to tell us what was in the parcel, eh? You're afraid we might do a bit of 'organizing' with it! Where d'you keep it, come on, when you're asleep."

"There was jam, a tin of tomatoes, condensed milk, biscuits . . ."

111

"Stop it! Tomatoes, Italian tomatoes, a tin with a white and red label I bet . . . You're killing us," I said, laughing.

"Come to my place sometime, I'll let you taste it!" And she began to move off, hesitant, broken.

"Great," I said, getting back into my bed again. "She'd've been better off if she hadn't got either letter or parcel. Like when they put you in prison and then bring you your first parcel from home. You look at the chicken and you can't eat it because you think of who cooked it for you and wrapped it up and suffered as they prepared it. Then you find some dry figs and you know they're there because Mom's remembered you're crazy about them. And then everything smells of home, they wanted it to be 'just like home,' and you cry and you can't eat it. You pick up one thing and then another and your stomach shrinks; you don't eat anything and you feel your strength draining away from you."

"That letter as well," Olga said. "With everything it didn't say . . ."

A week later Bianca Maria went into the hospital: erysipelas down one leg.

A month went by; the infection spread to the other leg. Bianca Maria read that one letter over and over and wept. "I'll never go back." Her friends went to see her and she sighed. "I'll never go back."

Every day she grew weaker, she wasted away, and the nostalgia, the yearning, the memories destroyed the last strength she had.

112

There Is a Place on Earth

—

No one ever felt more a prisoner than during the roll call, before dawn. The dark masses of the blocks, the dreary lines of women in their caps, the pale lights from the huts throwing a dark glow over small strips of earth—it all weighed down on our spirits. Even voices seemed to be toneless.

This oppressive ghostliness reminded us with tormenting insistence of our lost freedom and cruel fate. In that early morning hour it was destiny itself laid its powerful hands on our shoulders and tried to thrust us to the ground.

In the dark the boundary of the camp seemed to close in; beyond the barbed wire, night had swallowed up the outside world.

Lost in this state of mind, I didn't immediately hear my name and number being called out by the *bloccova*. Olga answered, and her arm pushed me forward from the line.

A name presupposes an individuality and a social existence; it belongs to the person it refers to the way a part of your body belongs to you. But we had lost our names, from the moment the dark stain of our numbers had been tattooed onto our left arms. Together with that name our dangerous and absurd individuality was supposed to disappear. The clothes we wore had disguised us and standardized us, and hunger, tiredness, and a kind of madness had given our already transformed faces the same absent or crazed expression.

Giuliana Tedeschi

That morning, the sky slowly growing lighter, my
name seemed to leap up from a distant by-now-
nonexistent world. My legs felt weak; I tried to
tense my muscles to stop the twitch that was shaking my shoulders. I was told to go to the *Büro*—
something new that had never happened to any of
us. From the expressions of my companions and the
way they said goodbye, I knew they shared my fear.
And when I saw them all setting off and I was left
alone, an instinctive need to prepare myself, to de-
fend myself, started me thinking of all the awful
things that might be about to happen.

"Perhaps," I thought, "it's to tell me my husband's dead." But I immediately rejected that pos-
sibility: such a thing would have been too merciful,
too humane for the Germans.

I was led into the office by an interpreter. An SS
man was sitting at the desk and didn't look up at
me. The interpreter handed me a postcard. Deeply
moved, I recognized the familiar handwriting of my
brother-in-law. I read the lines twice and every
word, every flourish of the writing was stamped on
my mind, as if photographed. The girls, my little
girls, who I'd left in danger, hiding, were safe! And
these few lines, these bare, essential facts, brought
back all my anxious searching for my family, the
eternal question as to what our fate would be—desperation and hope—and it was as if I was linked to
them by a thread. A call had come for me from the
outside world, it had managed to penetrate the
camp boundary; there was a force that was trying to

tear me away from this place, a force that would give me the energy to survive.

I kept all this inside me. I mustn't give anything away to this German, eager for information, for other victims to snatch, other prey to hunt down in whatever corner of Europe they were hiding. The interpreter was a prisoner; she understood, and when the German asked her to ask me who had sent the card, she translated, "It's an acquaintance of yours, right, sending you a card from Switzerland."

"An acquaintance, of course," I answered, and only then, looking at the signature, did I realize that it actually had been signed in the name of a Swiss friend, and that the card, addressed to a camp near here in a completely blind attempt to find me, had miraculously reached my camp and come to me among thousands upon thousands of other prisoners.

But my family would never know I'd received it, that I owed to that card a large part of my will to survive.

I was a bit light-headed when I came out of the *Büro;* most of the morning was still ahead of me, and I went to the open space between the blocks and the fence where grass poked out here and there in the stony clay.

Stretched on the ground, ragged bodies were soaking up the sun, amazed at this privilege. Every now and then a German in uniform would come by, snarling and swinging his belt; irritated, stumbling, the women fearfully gathered themselves and their rags together and wandered off to look for some other refuge.

It was a strange and unusual sight, these idle women out in the sunshine in a work camp.

They were prisoners kept behind, like myself, in the camp that day for some special reason and thus exonerated from work until tomorrow. I chose a place where I could at least rest my head on a few blades of grass. A tall woman was crouched down next to me. In the pallor of her face, two big, deep, black eyes were the only sign of energy and life. Her eyebrows likewise were black as could be, thick and straight beneath a high, smooth forehead, and a down of black hair had been allowed to invade the corners of her mouth. She pulled a piece of filthy cloth from a little bag and held it in her lap. Then she took a penknife from her pocket and untied the corners of her bundle. The blade flashed in the sun and the woman hummed a song under her breath. It was a pleasant tune with French words.

"Française?" I asked, happy to be able to talk to someone. The day was bright and warm; I hadn't worked, and felt communicative.

"Oui, Paris." The woman smiled, and she began to sing again. On her lap were some potato or turnip peels, some roots, and some almost rotten sticks of greens. With her knife she cut away the rotten parts, scraped, then put the pieces in her mouth, where they squeaked under her teeth.

"Careful that stuff doesn't make you sick!"

"Oh, I'm so hungry! He's eating me up. I feel

exhausted all the time, I can scarcely walk. And I have to think of feeding him as well as myself."

I looked at her, trying to understand, then realized that beneath the sloppy clothes, her body was beginning to take on the shape of pregnancy.

"Do you work?" I asked.

"No, not yet, luckily enough. I'm in a quarantine block for scarlet fever." She brought a handful of peels to her lips while her hands went on quickly scraping the waste scraps.

She had that trusting calm about her that pregnancy brings. I said nothing, since I thought questions would upset her. The calm way her hands moved, it was as if she were knitting.

"And then it'll be over, *chérie*. My husband said it would be over in August. The English have landed, soon they'll be in Paris!"

"When is the baby due?"

"In December, four more months. I think I can make it and then . . . we'll be in France and he'll be born in Paris, in a new world . . ."

I was deeply moved, my eyes bright.

"Cheer up, cheer up," she said, squeezing my arm, interpreting my emotion as weakness. "We'll make it back, I'm sure we will." Saying which, she got up and set off confidently toward the huts.

A new trainload had arrived from Italy—more friends and relations in that tragic corner of the earth!

Going into the block where the most recent arrivals were housed, I held my breath. Who would I

117

find among those shy, unsuspecting women with their sad eyes, huddling together in the bunks. All at once a shape moved, slithered down from her bunk, and was standing before me, tall, healthy. Before I could even get out her name, I felt the warmth of her body against mine, her arms around my neck.

"Who did you come with?" I asked my cousin, Natalia, and my voice was hesitant.

"With Mother and Grandmother," the girl said calmly. "But they went to the other end of the road, to another camp, and we came here."

I couldn't speak, my knowledge crushed me.

"They'll be with Aunt Norina." Natalia meant my husband's mother. "They won't be alone."

"Right," I answered without looking at her. "They'll be together, they'll be together . . . But, remember now, you must eat, always, even if the soup is horrible, save as much of your energy as you can, and above all you must want to live . . ."

From outside came the cry of *"Lagersperre,"* and I rushed out of the block to join thirty or so girls running to the gates to get back into Camp B.

The gate that separated Camp A from Camp B had already been closed. In front of it the *Blockführer*, arms folded, face inscrutable, was staring at a group of women standing still and hesitant in front of him. Suddenly, he showed his teeth and narrowed his eyes, his head leaning forward in a brutal, sadistic sneer. We shuddered, we tensed our legs, which had begun to tremble, and our faces filled with fear. The German clenched his fists, he bent a leg, and he hurled himself on this defenseless bunch with the fury of a beast.

The group broke up amid cries and groans. The man attacked again, fists held high, striking out blindly with feet and hands. We ran about, trying to hide behind each other, arms over our eyes so as not to see that fixed sneer and the cap with the skull just a few inches from our faces.

"Die Nummern einschreiben!" the *Blockführer* finally yelled to the *Lagerkapo* who was standing nearby. Now it was the woman's turn. She was one of those sexless monsters the Germans had bred specially for the concentration camps, stiff and wooden in her black blouse, hair cut like a man's, the hoarse voice of a drinker.

Her hand came down heavily on each of our cheeks. At the end of the camp, smoke rose from the crematoriums against a sunset red sky. "They're taking us to the crematorium!" my sick, haunted nerves told me. "They're writing the numbers to take us to the crematorium!" I thought of my husband, my daughters, my home far away, and resignation overcame my pang of remorse: "It had to happen."

Later, in the cozy warmth of the bunk, Olga commented: "Mad!"

"Yes, sometimes you feel you're close to insanity," I answered. That night I dreamed of a broad staircase and at the end, on the left, a large, low redbrick buiding with a curved wall. All around was pleasant countryside—rustling birches and bushes, fields and avenues. Mother was in the garden and wanted to go into the building, and I was below at the foot of the stairs shouting and waving to her not to go in. But I couldn't speak; the words wouldn't come from my mouth. She was crying and calling me and I knew, but I couldn't stop her going in . . . I woke up. In the bunk next to mine Dina was fretting and moaning in her sleep. "Mama," she was calling . . .

"Dina doesn't know," Olga whispered. "We won't tell her. Her mother was on the last train and she hasn't come into the camp. And did you hear? Zilly's daughter too."

"Good night, dear. My daughter is your age . . ." Zilly's voice echoed in my mind.

13

At
Reveille

Masses of clouds, swollen and gray, cross the sky, collide with each other, slide over and under each other, melt, spread. The sky seems to lower over the huts, becomes dark and uniform; there are dull rumbles, the storm breaks. The rain comes down in torrents; it has weight and volume and forms a quivering moving curtain in front of your eyes. The even, constant pelting mingles with the trickling of gutters. In a few minutes the camp has been transformed into a bog: the dry, cracked clay soaks up the water and becomes squelchy and slippery.

The roll call goes on; no matter what, the roll call

goes on. This indifference to obstacles both human and natural is a display of power on the Germans' part.

Lined up immobile in front of our blocks, we feel our feet slowly sinking into the miry ground and getting firmly stuck there. Our sodden clothes no longer offer any protection and the raindrops run down our bodies with a cool tickling feel. The rain beats heavily on our foreheads and cheeks, trickles through our hair and kerchiefs.

The line of women sways uncertainly as people attempt to get some shelter against the walls. But the *bloccova* yells for them to move back into the bog. There's nothing that isn't drenched, no one who doesn't now feel in her heart that she is the undeserving victim of both man and nature.

When the pelting eases up and the air clears, the sky lifts and is light again. From the roads between the blocks, the black cloaks and pointed caps of the *Aufseherinnen* reappear, swaying on their boots.

The line has reformed and awaits the cold scrutiny of the enemy's inspection. At last we can go back into the block for the whole of Sunday afternoon.

We run to our mattresses the way an animal returns to its lair. But after a few moments the humidity from outside has penetrated the hut. Wherever they come to rest, your hands draw back at the unpleasant sensation of stickiness and dampness. The planks of the bunk beds, where soaking clothes have been hung in a jumble, become impregnated with water. The brick floor is covered with the sludge stuck to everybody's clogs. Naked bodies shiver and clutch blankets to themselves, desperate for softness and warmth, but the blankets are already damp, and too rough to cling and give warmth.

The next morning your body warm with the night's sweat, you pull on the same wet rags with a sense of discomfort and distress that turns your skin to gooseflesh.

—

For seven days the road to the *Schuhkommando* danced before my eyes. The hazy, indistinct countryside quivered, and the movement of ten pairs of legs in front of me blurred my vision and made me feel seasick. For seven days I clenched my teeth and gathered all my strength to keep myself upright on my work stool. The hours passed slowly. Amid the deafening clamor of the hut the whine in my ears became something distinct, solidifying my own silence, the physical silence of a body that can no longer respond. My head burned and fell sideways on my shoulder, my fingers slowed down, shoes and scissors would slip from my hand for a moment at once brief and long as eternity. My whole being slipped down into a torpid drowsiness until a call from my companions warned me the *Aufseherin* or the *Posten* were coming, and with a start and a twinge I would painfully fight my way back to consciousness.

One damp, dark dawn, in the toilet hut, under the uncertain glow of the distant perimeter lights, an atmosphere heavy with humanity and filth, I started to faint. The ground seemed to slope away under my feet. I managed a few hurried steps to my left and grabbed hold of a friend.

A little later, getting up from my bunk, I had the same feeling of unsteadiness spreading out from ears and stomach and forcing me to grab the planks of the bunk for support. It was time to give in, to go to the hospital, accept the risk of a selection. There was anxiety in the quick handshake with my fellow prisoners, anxiety in their eyes as they weighed up my ruined face, then looked away more gloomy than before. But after so many days of fever my own anxiety had been transformed into resignation and surrender. I had no regrets, though when I saw all the others going out, turning to wave to me at the corner of the block, when I watched as they were lost in the melee of so many thousands of women lining up to go to work, it felt as though I were standing there naked by the door of the hut. And I felt I was alone for the first time, perhaps to remain alone forever. Prison life is like a piece of knitting whose stitches are strong as long as they remain woven together; but if the woolen strand breaks, the invisible stitch that comes undone slips off among the others and is lost.

From seven till ten a group of feverish women shivered in front of the admission hut, clutching their rags around them and stamping their clogs on the ground while the wind lashed painfully at burning limbs.

The admission area was the anteroom of one of the hospital wards; by the big open door we were still in direct contact with the cold air outside. There was an indescribable stench of pus, mold, medicine, chamber pots, and feverish humanity. Here, for a few moments, the prisoners laid bare the misery of their flesh: the huge sunburn sores, the big purplish boils of vitamin deficiency scattered over legs and buttocks, the infected cuts that impoverished blood could no longer close and heal.

They were given zinc oxide or Ichthyol ointments and a paper bandage that soon fell off, leaving wounds once again exposed to infection and painful irritation.

By the time they had checked my fever, looked at my tongue and throat, and decided to put me in the influenza ward, I dreamed of nothing better than a small strip of straw mattress to stretch my aching limbs on.

Instead, my clothes and shoes taken away from me in the anteroom of the ward, barefoot and naked among a dozen or so patients, I waited on the stone platform that ran the length of the block for the ward doctor to do her rounds and assign me a bed. My still-young body had already lost a lot of weight; my left breast was pulsing fast with fever, my legs trembled, my weak wrists hung limp. It was only by calling on the last ounce of mental strength that I managed to climb, teeth chattering, trembling, up to the highest bunk. Stretched out, my body relaxed in abandon and repose! Shuddering at the contact with the empty mattress and the rough blanket, I lay in a state of semiconsciousness. From then on my sensations were confused, reaching me from an alien world through the barrier of a constantly high fever. There was the terrible *"Aufstehen"* shouted in the still-pitch dark after a sleepless night; the icy water of the basin where I had to wash completely naked amid biting drafts; the beads of sweat on my forehead as I struggled to climb back to my bed; the sudden knocking on the scaffolding of the bunk disturbing feverish drowsing when the nurses brought around the bread, or the soup, or the thermometer.

And the nights! The interminable nights, lying immersed in an icy perspiration that soaked nightdress and blanket, breathing the cold air that came straight down from the skylight, pressing hands against a tired heavy heart! The nights, which the nurses' chatter, the rinsing of their underwear in basins, the smell of their food cooking on the stove, the moans and shouts of the other patients, filled with nightmares!

Artillery fire rumbled in the distance; there were the explosions of bombs dropping close by, while from immediately behind the row of hospital huts came the booming of wagon wheels on rails, the shriek of brakes, and the clamor of thousands of new arrivals.

The drowsiness produced by the fever, by general weakness, and by aspirin dulled our sensibility to suffering and even death. My eyes were slow and indifferent as they followed the half-naked body of an old Polish woman, an Aryan, who had died during the night and was being taken from her bed and then dragged along the ground, held by her armpits. The nurse rummaged around in the still-warm mattress eagerly hunting for any leftover bread. Before long another sufferer was already in there. And along the stone platform in the center of the hut, exhausted bodies stood and waited, bodies that could scarcely breathe, wheezing and moaning, heaps of bones wrapped in wrinkled skin, skeletons with nothing human about them anymore.

It was while I was in hospital that something epic happened in the camp, an episode that was to pass from mouth to mouth and become a legend.

"You don't know Mala," said those who had been in the camp the longest, "a charming girl. Two years ago, when she'd only just arrived from Belgium, the Germans called her out at roll call and chose her to work in the *Büro* . . ."

". . . she never had to do any heavy work and she had important responsibilities . . . the Germans treated her well . . ."

One late afternoon, the sun still tingeing the clouds with red, the Jewish work parties coming back through the gate were told to line up along the main road. The Aryans hurried back to their huts and were forbidden to leave them.

Panic spread among the Jewish women, who immediately feared a general selection.

In the middle of the camp, with the sky as backdrop, a gallows was erected. After a few minutes, escorted by SS officials, a small, dark, extremely pale woman appeared and walked between the lines of prisoners.

". . . the German officer began to speak . . ." And it's here that the story ceases to be simple fact and becomes pretty well legend. "We couldn't hear very clearly. He was saying that anyone who attempted, like Mala, to escape would die like her on the gallows . . ."

"Right, you know what happened? A month ago Mala had managed to escape with the help of a Polish prisoner who knew the area . . ."

"Yes, yes, he was in love with her. He was from around here, and since he knew the language, it wasn't difficult for him . . ."

"They say they organized it brilliantly: they left the camp dressed as SS . . ."

"Just think, they were living for a month hidden up in the farmers huts up in the hills . . ."

"They even hid their numbers with iodine and sticking plaster."

"And they got themselves caught at the Czech border, trying to get across . . ."

"No, they say it was in a luxury nightclub . . ."

When the German officer had finished (and here people's stories become less fantastic and more similar), just as the second part of the ceremony was about to begin, Mala suddenly made a move and— before anyone could stop her or even realized what she was about to do—she slapped the German right across the face, shouting, "It won't be you that kills me; Mala will kill herself!" And taking out a razor blade, she swiftly cut her veins and lay in a faint in her own blood. Everybody looked on, proud and moved, while the rope dangled pointlessly from the gallows.

Her body was taken straight to the hospital and in the meantime the Germans quickly gave the order for the prisoners to go back to their huts.

"They saved her and then sent her to the crematorium . . ."

At the same time, in the men's camp, the Polish prisoner was hung.

—

At last one day the fever passes. Luciana is in a hurry to discharge me because she's afraid there may be a selection. I file naked before a German officer to get myself discharged.

His look comes from far off, it seems to travel an enormous way to reach my miserable body; he has to put a very big distance indeed between a pure Aryan SS officer and a filthy Jewish prisoner.

I stagger out of the hospital door under a gray blanket. The shower and then the block again, the same block, thank heaven!

That evening among friends in our bunks and the next day on my stool at work, it's as if I had rediscovered a tiny harbor.

Everything is the same—nature, the huts, the shoes to take to pieces.

14

"Next Year in Jerusalem"

Every voice had been hushed in the dark of the gathering. There had been a moment of general emotion, the girls had hugged and kissed each other, the Greeks in the upper beds had sought out the Italians below. Everyone had felt their souls go out to embrace the suffering of the others along with their own, had felt their own hopes mingle with everybody's hopes, beyond all barriers and national divisions.

"Next New Year at home!" It was the evening of Rosh Hashanah, the Jewish New Year. "In Greece, in Italy!" said the Greeks, and this aspiration echoed the traditional saying that expresses our eternal hope: *"L'shanah ha-ba'ah b'yerushalayim* —Next year in Jerusalem."

Even the Poles who slept to the right had shouted something in German from their beds.

The women reached their mattresses. The most intimate moment had arrived, when at home the family gathers around for the lighting of the ritual seven-branched candlestick. Four, five, ten little candles, stubs stolen from work, were lit and stuck with a drop of wax to the Greeks' beds. The little flames burnt tremblingly, shyly, sadly, and in the spaces between the beds the light wavered.

Staring into the source of the light, our eyes focused on that dark, secret point that seemed to hide within itself our memory of the past, until our eyelids closed to hold back the tears.

Then the Greeks began their lament, like some archaic wail of bereavement: their voices would settle for a long time on the same note with monotonous insistence and primitive satisfaction, then break out into sobs.

Sitting on their beds, the Polish women rocked back and forth as is their way, looking at the occasional prayer book stolen by the Canada party from the luggage of the deportees, softly singing the day's prayers to their traditional tune.

Doubtless my father, exile as he was, would be bent forward over his well-thumbed book of prayers, finding in the eternal words of the page he had read every year at Rosh Hashanah some comfort in the face of the tragedy that had befallen his family . . .

"Enough!" Olga screamed, turning around, suffocated by this atmosphere of tragic tradition. "If these Greeks don't shut up . . . I can't stand it!"

15

Auschwitz!

For some months a rumor had been going around that the *Schuhkommando* and any other parties that had to walk from Birkenau to Auschwitz to work would be moved to the Auschwitz camp, where some new women's blocks were being built.

It happened quite suddenly. Late one afternoon coming back from work, our party was given the order not to go back into the block but to head directly for the *Sauna*, the hut with the showers.

Knotted together, our clothes were put through the steam cleaner while we lined up naked ready to file by in front of a medical officer and a nurse.

As soon as the women saw their own defenseless bodies, worried eyes began to gauge their leanness. "Am I too thin?" they all asked each other.

"I've got spots on my breast . . . as long as they don't think it's scabies . . ."

There wasn't a single limb of a single body that didn't tremble at the thought that this was a form of selection: The ones who passed muster went to Auschwitz, the others God knew where. Standing stiff, heads held high, the women filed before the cold eyes of the Germans, hiding their nudity behind hatred and scorn. No sooner had they got past than they were fearing for the thin, pale, stumbling companions behind them.

Dina was stopped. Her hunched shoulders, her breasts, once florid, now hollow and withered, the typically sharp nose and yellowish, transparent ears, could fool no one.

"Pulmonary tuberculosis," said the German, making her stand to one side. Thus Dina, German-Jewish refugee, heard her sentence in her own language.

The already scanty group of Italians, or of those who, despite being foreign refugees, spoke Italian, was now down to three—Olga, Vicky, and myself. We lost Dina, who stayed behind in Birkenau, and Ruth, who had been forced into the hospital with pneumonia, and all the others who worked in the other parties.

We waited for the *Entlausung,* the monthly disinfection, one of the most feared means of persecution carried out in the name of hygiene.

"One more *Entlausung,* or maybe two, and then . . ." said the women every month. But one month ran into the next—six had already passed since we had arrived in Birkenau in April—and the war had not ended.

From the warm shower room the women walked streaming with water into the huge cold room next to it where air flowed in through the many glassless windows. It was a long wait, the whole night, before our clothes emerged; then they came out of the steam cleaner, still boiling hot and as dirty as before, but disinfected. Meanwhile our naked, shivering bodies, exhausted by the lack of food and overcome by weariness and sleep, would gradually sink to the ground one on top of another in a huge shapeless mass of flesh where heads mingled with stomachs and legs got tangled up with other legs.

Against the wall, in a corner, alone and unable to sleep, I trembled at that spectacle of appalling wretchedness and neglect, awaiting the dawn and my clothes.

—

The Birkenau women were lined up for a roll call in Auschwitz, waiting to go into their new block.

"Look at their eyes," said the Auschwitz girls, walking by, "dilated, lost—terrified eyes, mad eyes . . ." The Birkenau women were stunned, shocked; an enchanted world was opening up before them. No more huts, but proper two-story buildings with spacious dormitories where huge bunk beds with colored quilted blankets lined the walls. The washroom was inside the block on the first floor; the toilets were English-style, proper lavatories with chains and a flush! Then in the semibasement, tables and stools created the illusion of a dining hall. No one went to bed that evening without having felt the excitement of pulling the lavatory chain two or three times, without having dried their faces in a clean towel, without having admired themselves, after so many months, in a clean, feminine nightdress. It was all so exciting—sitting on a stool, putting your bread on a table, the swaying gait and fleshy thighs of the *Lagerkapo* . . . And the crematorium out of sight, no longer ever-present, always, always there.

How come Birkenau next to Auschwitz? Why did thousands and thousands of people have to die in Birkenau, while only a few could live in Auschwitz? It was one of the many enigmas. Perhaps Auschwitz was destined to appear to the world at the end of the war as a model camp, after Birkenau and all its crematoriums had been blown up by dynamite?

The new beds with their ample, wide mattresses welcomed the weary women, and at dawn the siren for reveille woke them an hour later than they were used to.

An Indian summer hung on in Poland through that September of 1944. It breathed a subdued atmosphere of expectancy, a mute foreboding of something that is dying, breaking down. The sky was blue and fiery at sundown. The rich countryside had that satisfied repose, that sense of reward and respite that follows the period of maximum fertility. The trees still had their foliage and nests. Everything seemed static and immobile, and only every now and then a fresh little breeze brought a sniff of autumn.

The artillery had fallen silent for quite a few days now; there had been no drone of engines in the air, no warning sirens. The Germans themselves had a milder look to them, sometimes their faces had the smile of someone who is looking forward to the coziness of home life again, and when they spoke, the words *nach Hause* were frequently on their lips.

"They're negotiating a peace treaty," the prisoners said. "Seems they've already agreed on fourteen points . . ." And nature appeared to coddle them with this hope.

"Wars always finish in autumn," they said. "You don't suppose they want to go through another winter, with the enemy at their borders. Winter is about keeping warm, covering yourself up, eating . . ."

For us too, especially for us in fact, winter meant keeping warm, covering up, eating.

"*A la maison pour la Noël,*" said the French. "*A Natale in Italia . . .*" we repeated.

"They said something about peace," whispered a prisoner one morning. Mirale and a *Posten*. They said, "*Frieden,*" and laughed.

The days went monotonously by. Nothing of the turmoil going on in the outside world leaked

137

through to us. In the *Schuhkommando* hut we pulled shoes to pieces without end; at work, in the toilets, in the dormitories, we wallowed in forecasts and invented utopian solutions.

"You know," the women said more confidently, getting together in small groups, "There's been an order from Berlin to stop the gassing. It's the end, the end . . ."

Then one day the grumble of artillery fire broke the pregnant silence.

"It's nearer," whispered the women, looking at each other, and the air-raid siren began to wail. Thus every hope of imminent peace was dashed and the images of home and family dissolved like fog. The war went on with all its destructive fury. It got closer; it would overwhelm us, bury us.

Two miles from Auschwitz, Birkenau was still there and at Birkenau everything had remained as it was. Birkenau existed to suffocate hope and annihilate logic, to provoke madness and death. Bianca, who had been working as a doctor at the hospital for eight months, was at the limits of her mental resistance. For four days, since the ghoulish figure of Dr. Mengele had been doing the rounds of her wards, she had neither slept nor eaten.

In the "death block" at the far end of the hospital, fifty prisoners chosen in the selection were waiting to be taken to the crematorium at any moment. Fifty desperate, crazed faces, a hundred wide eyes, yells and tears and then . . . Why go on living and treating patients in the hospital? If only she had died, unsuspecting, in the crematorium with her parents and sister right after they arrived! But at the last moment a German officer had said, "Any doctors, out!" and that had saved her.

Fifty human beings knowing they were going to die, shut up like beasts in a cage, with every hour, every breath living their last. Many of the women were ready to leave this world perhaps, but no one wanted to accept this kind of death.

Two were Italians, friends of Bianca's. Laura was a small, naturally delicate woman, but healthy. She had big, black intelligent eyes, a good, clean face. She had not cried.

"Bianca," was all she had whispered, trembling, "if you get back to Italy, maybe you will get back, go to my husband and my mother . . ."

Wanda was young, she hadn't finished school yet, not much more than a bundle of skin and bones. She had clung to her friend's neck. "Bianca, save me, save me!" she yelled. "I don't want to die. I'm going mad, I'm going mad!" Her hands sunk into Bianca's neck like claws.

With those cries in her ears Bianca ran to the medicine cabinet. She looked around. She opened it quickly, took out a tube, and hid it in her bust. Then she waited for night to fall. The camp was dark and silent. She sneaked out of the block alone and, hugging the walls of the huts, reached the last "death block." At a closed window, she called, "Laura, Laura, Wanda!" A feeble voice answered from inside. "Take it, it's a strong sleeping medicine." A hand came out between the bars and disappeared inside.

Her hands on her stomach, Bianca ran as far as her own bed and threw herself down on her back.

—

Suddenly, insistently, the alarm siren rent the air. But the noise didn't go up or down at regular intervals, nor was there any drone of engines in the distance, nor sound of exploding bombs.

Mirale rushed wildly into the hut, her cap askew. The women looked at her anxiously, eyelids fluttering.

"Quick! In line," shouted Mirale hoarsely. "*Antreten!*"

The shrill, incessant sound found an echo in our heads, making us nervous and hurried as we spoke and moved. We reached the camp at a run and the gate was closed behind us. All the work parties were wandering around in a confused crowd outside their blocks.

"They've gassed two hundred men in the *Sonderkommando,* the damned pigs! The women in Birkenau who work in the Canada party said so."

"Right, but that's not why the siren's on."

One morning the women in the Canada group had gone to work as usual. They opened the disinfection chamber—everything upside down, all over the place, and a faint smell of almonds still in the air. The men's struggle had been appalling and in vain.

"Two hundred men of the *Sonderkommando,*"

the women said, the special party that worked in the crematorium. All of them destined to die; they knew too much. The Germans said, "Take these blankets and carry them to the disinfection room in the Canada hut." And they took the blankets and put them down in the room. But as soon as they were in there, the door closed behind them. There was no other opening and the gas came in. Men instead of bugs and fleas.

"Okay, so they won't be gassing anymore," we all thought, while a sense of emptiness gripped our stomachs; we felt we couldn't breathe, were about to faint.

"But why the alarm siren now? What can have happened?" No one knew what it was, only that something must have happened.

The great news went around the whole camp with the speed of lightning. The toilets and showers, dormitories and work parties, were full of it. It was so mind-boggling, so unexpected, that no one who had heard it could stop themselves from sharing it with someone else, anybody else.

"One of the Birkenau crematoriums has been blown up! The survivors of the *Sonderkommando* did it."

"Half the building is a heap of rubble! The gas chamber has been destroyed." The sad flame would no longer rise from the central chimney, the dark, constant threat that had until now dominated the camp. Moved, the men and women felt like survivors.

A week later the *Union*, the party that worked in

141

the munitions factory, was in turmoil. The women stopped in groups in the toilets, in the washrooms, in the corridors of the blocks.

"They've been investigating. They've taken away four people, four Polish girls who worked the night shift."

"What did they do? Why?"

"They took away the powder, that's the rumor, a bit at a time, and they put earth in the shells."

"Great!"

"Right, but now they'll pay for it. You know when they blew up the gas chamber in the crematorium? That was the powder they used. The women had passed it on to the men. Now they're shut up in the *Bunker!*"

"Oh God, what will happen?"

16

Sandgruben

On the railway line outside the *Schuhkommando*
six freight wagons stood and waited. The women
didn't sit down on their stools this morning. The
old *Schuhkommando* was being wound up; the material was to be taken away to safety in Germany.
"Did you see yesterday," the women were saying,
"those two civilians, an old man and a young one?
They were talking to Mirale. The Russians have
advanced too fast these last months, and they're
afraid they might lose this mountain of filthy shoes.
They want to have them all back in Germany!"
  A thin rain was melting the snow and turning the

road into a freezing bog. In pairs the women picked up the wooden cases, went into the store hut in a long line, loaded the cases with shoes, and took them to the wagons where other women standing above emptied them.

From seven in the morning till six in the evening, the work went on without a break, becoming more and more frenetic. The snow, mixed with water, had already penetrated our shoes, and by now the rain was gluing our clothes to our bodies.

"All summer," the women said, "we suffocated in that scorching hut without a breath of air. But this winter we would have been working in the dry . . ."

"You'll see, there's nothing left for us now but to die of cold out in the *Aussenkommando* . . ." and they watched nostalgically as the hut emptied of shoes.

At six o'clock two of the wagons were still empty. The *Aufseherin* screamed; no one would be going back until the wagons were loaded. The exhausted women looked at the mud and their aching feet. It was an act of heroism on behalf of the whole party. Everybody got their breath, picked up their cases. No one spoke to their partners anymore; all they had before them were shoes, shoes that tumbled down from the walls in the huts and shoes that piled up in the wagons. The women helped each other in the dark, calling to each other, going ahead in long lines to gain time, organizing the way the work was divided up.

By ten o'clock all the wagons were full. The party was exhausted; we still hadn't had our bread ration. But the excitement of exhaustion couldn't be calmed all at once. In the dark the women started to walk, and they spoke with one voice, a warm voice raised in the darkness, deep and mysterious.

The *Schuhkommando* had shut up shop. It was the *Aussenkommando* for us now: work outside in midwinter.

—

"I almost feel like the bandit of the Casbah," said Olga, gesturing to the landscape.

Along the horizon were the lines of camouflaged camp blocks. On this side of the camp, crossed by a road that led to the village, were two enormous sand pits, the *Sandgruben*. The country looked like something from a film. The ground fell sharply away from high canyon walls of still-untouched sand and huge heaps of soil; it became confused in twists and turns, was choked with tracks, gullies, and trenches. Beyond the pits rose the barbed-wire fence with the *Postens'* watchtowers.

Equipped with shovels, we went down into a trench. A lucky trench! The sides were too high for us to be seen and a high quarry wall, above which ran the perimeter track, kept us out of sight of the *Posten* in his little wooden tower.

The party working in the pits was made up of women from the parties that had been disbanded for lack of work. There were Greeks, Poles, Hungarians, and French, but we were in the Latin section—everybody was French or Italian. The Greeks, noisy and argumentative, scattered in groups to work in the holes farthest away, and the Hungarians, with their whining way of talking that sounded to us like the meowing of melancholy cats, all got together in an area they kept for themselves.

"Allô, mes enfants!" Julian threw her shovel against the wall of sand that rose above our heads in front of us. "This wall is our salvation! Death to whoever touches it, to whoever takes so much as a shovelful of sand! Hear the wind up there? It lashes at you; it goes right through your clothes." The wind was master in that boundless plain where neither woods nor hills obstructed its path.

"Vous savez, mes filles," what I'm going to tell you," said Madame Robert in her singsong voice. "I'm telling you we're not going to die. It's the end of October, the winter is long, but we're not going to die." And she hopped back and forth, raising the collar of her tattered coat and hiding her ears under her cap. With her round eyes and thin sticklike legs, she looked like an old plucked hen.

The job of *Vorarbeiterin* had gone to Edith. Her figure heavy and swollen with the last months of pregnancy, she climbed up high onto an earthen ledge. She acted as a lookout for the others so that she wouldn't have to lift the heavy shovel or pick.

"And for you, Madame Paul," said Thérèse, "another responsible job—to watch over the toilet." This was a favor conceded to the oldest of the prisoners.

"And in case you didn't know, Madame Paul," Charlotte shouted after her, "the toolshed's near the lav. You can keep a bit warmer in there."

"Vingt-deux," warned Edith from above. The shovels hurried with a sudden clamor, striking alternately. The German in charged appeared on a rampart.

"He's gone," said Edith a few minutes later. The shovels stopped, were thrust into the sand or propped under an armpit to lean on.

"Julian!" I called.

"Oui," she answered from the other end. She had pushed back her cap a bit, and you could see her lovely blond, wavy hair above a high, smooth forehead.

"Julian, listen to this." I drew my breath and whistled the opening tune of Beethoven's Fifth.

First Julian's confident whistle joined mine, then Olga's voice, slightly out of tune, and a breath of life wafted over the sad alien meanders of the pits. It was the most moving concert of our lives. From the heroic, impassioned symphonies of Beethoven we went on to the mournful, tender melodies of Mozart's piano concertos; then from Mozart to the clear voices of Bach's arias and *Lieder*, to return finally to the grandoise humanity of Beethoven's sonatas.

"Vingt-deux." We heard Edith's voice and re-

sponded with unusual fervor. The work began again.

From the edge of the pit the supervisor shouted, *"Antreten!"*

The morning was over before we could have hoped, the resources of the spirit had beaten the cold, and when the hot soup raised body heat and confidence, everybody was excited to find that they were sure they could stick it out.

—

We were coming back from work and the camp was already in sight.

"See that hut," Sara said to me, pointing to a building facing the camp, "my husband works there. It's the tailors' hut. When we go by, he looks out the window."

As soon as we were in the camp, Sara ran and, standing tall near the fence, raised a hand.

In the workshop a slender man sitting on a stool was looking out the window. He was apparently immobile but not relaxed, his torso erect, all the muscles of his face tense. He kept his legs tucked under the stool, as if they might have to move suddenly. He didn't nod his head or move a hand. Once he had done so and they had beaten him. But no one could stop his eyes looking, and behind the eyes his soul.

Sara was there; he could make out her small black figure with the arm still held high. The woman glimpsed a seated shape, imagined rather

than saw him, imagined his features in the most
minute detail. Everyday, together with a surge of
affection, she would feel herself filled with certainty. "We're still alive. Alive, both of us, and we
know it."

In the evening, sitting on her mattress, she undid
a worn-out wool stocking.

"It's for him, to protect his ears against the cold,"
she confided to me. "I'm going to send it to him
through a friend. Next week it's his birthday!"

I was overwhelmed by a sense of pity and tenderness. I envied her expression of contentment
and joy, her busy, excited hands. Everything about
her had the echo of a lost well-being: the pleasure
of giving a present! Dear God, to know nothing of
him, nothing of my husband!

—

"Tante Berthe, where have you got to?" Olga was
calling around the dormitory. "Tante Berthe, a letter for you!" She waved a folded sheet of paper.

"What?" I asked, running into her.

"Yes, a letter from Tante Berthe's son. A man
gave it to me at work this morning."

"Let me see," I said, grabbing her arm. The
folded sheet of paper and a few lines of man's handwriting had made us feel nervous and excited.

I went to the *Waschraum*, the toilets, climbed the
stairs, came back down again. Tante Berthe was
standing in the middle of a group of prisoners. Her
tall figure and good-natured face were familiar;

since arriving from France and getting into the camp by sheer miracle—for she wasn't young—she had been with us in the *Schuhkommando* and now again in the *Sandgruben.*

"Tante Berthe, quick," I shouted, running to her. "We've been looking for you for ages. There's a letter for you, a letter from your son."

"Where, where?" the poor woman faltered; her slack cheeks flushed red, and her chin and the loose skin on her neck began to tremble slightly.

"Quick, Olga's got it, let's go."

She hugged me. I was in as much of a hurry as she was, a hurry to share her joy and emotion, to hear her news, as if the letter belonged a little bit to me too. Later, stretched on her bed, Olga told me, "That letter, I couldn't help it, it was open and I read it before giving it to her. I haven't seen a sheet of paper with writing for centuries."

"So? News about the war? What does he think?" I asked, and I wasn't surprised by her indiscretion. The letter belonged to us, we had the right to it too, and I wanted to know what was in it as soon as possible.

"It didn't say much. The news is good, everything okay, stick it out and in a couple of months . . ."

"Oh right, in two or three months . . ." I repeated the refrain, disbelieving.

"But if he says it, and he's a man . . . He's a doctor in the hospital, maybe there they do get some news . . ."

These vague words from an unknown man
slipped into our hearts and revived the hope that
time and the tough life of the camp were eroding
day by day with the insistence of water on stone.

There was a long silence between us, each of us
thinking her own thoughts.

"He called her *'petite maman chérie,'*" said
Olga. "The French language has such a rich range
of nuance for expressing feeling, love, passion . . ."

I sensed in this generic comment and in the faint-
est quiver in her voice the same desire for affection
and need for deep tenderness that rose to the surface more often in me, but which Olga hid behind
a determined toughness. We were close and quiet
together again when Tante Berthe came to our
bunk to tell us her news.

"Oh, *mes enfants,* we'll be going home soon,
everything's going okay. Yes, he says the news is
very good . . ." But we weren't listening; all we saw
was the change that had come across her face. It
was a face that had suffered a great deal, haggard,
gray, flabby, and baggy; except that now it was alive
with movement, had taken on color, and the lively
eyes moved from one face to another with excitement.

"*Ecoutez, mes enfants,* maybe I'll be able to see
him. I'll be able to see my son. He's been lucky:
they're using him as a doctor in the hospital in the
men's camp. I'll go to the men's camp next week
saying I need an X-ray. And I'll see him . . . Have I
changed a lot, what do you think? I was so fat be-

fore. I wouldn't like him to be upset when he sees me . . . Has anybody got a mirror, please?" Olga offered her a fragment of mirror.

"Of course not, Tante Berthe," I said. "Look at you, you look lovely today, Tante Berthe. He'll be proud of you." She looked at herself; twice her hand rose to adjust the kerchief knotted under her chin.

"It doesn't suit me, it makes me look old."

"*Alors, Tante Berthe, tenez*—try this," said Olga, throwing her her own kerchief, which had a lighter color. "You'll look fantastic." We laughed as Tante Berthe looked into the mirror and prepared a face to see her son.

—

"*Allô, mes enfants, faites attention!*" shouted Madame Paul, appearing from behind a heap of sand. "The *Posten* is *une sale vache* this morning!"

"*Que le diable l'emporte, le vieux chameau!*" shouted Olga and threw away her shovel.

For the moment everything was quiet. A few days ago Edith had switched to a party working inside and Thérèse had taken her place.

A long line of carts came back and forth along the main track through the pit and all the women had been rounded up to load the sand. Now the carts had gone and likewise the supervisor.

"*Prospère . . . houp là boum*," sang Thérèse from above, walking around with her hands in her pockets. Reassured by her singing, the others had dropped their shovels and huddled around Tante Berthe. It was our technique for defending ourselves from the cold.

"Tante Berthe, Tante Berthe, come on, tell us a little story!"

"*Pas maintenant, pas maintenant,*" Tante Berthe parried.

"Oh come on . . . Tante Berthe! Even your son loved your *'petites histoires drôles'.*"

"The Polish one about the Frenchwomen, Tante Berthe," said Julian.

Tante Berthe began; her voice took on a falsetto tone, a characteristic singsong, a mannered accent. The heat of the bodies huddled tightly around her tall figure slowly seeped into her. The laughter of the girls (and creating laughter is a rare conquest in a concentration camp) brightened her sharp black eyes, and a flare for comedy surfaced from amid the wrinkles of her flaccid, wasted face, an inexhaustible verve that had once made her company so precious to her friends, over dinner, at parties.

"*. . . il ramasse les billets . . . quel sacrifice . . .*" Thérèse went on singing, tapping one clog against another, a sign that all was calm.

"*Ah, mes filles,*" Tante Berthe concluded, laughing now herself, "I'm happy to be with you. It was a miracle . . . I got in here by the skin of my teeth."

"Tell us about that too, Tante Berthe!" everybody insisted.

"*Prospère . . . houp là . . . boum!*" came Thé-

earth, and sand; a piece of the parapet crumbled away and the wall was noticeably lower.

"Scheisse!" cried Olga, shaking the sand off her back. I looked at her in amazement. "Yes, I know you can't say it . . . When you're finally capable of getting satisfaction out of an obscenity," Olga said, looking at me seriously, "your spirit will be armored against camp life."

Some more earth fell.

"Merde alors! You're incapable of breaking through conventions."

"What have conventions got to do with it! What I can't do is give up my character," I protested heatedly.

"Okay, so you just go on saying 'Excuse me,' and 'Please' and 'Thank you' to the Poles and see where it gets you."

"It's like blowing your nose without a handkerchief," said Julian. "At first you hunt around desperately for a rag, a corner torn off a shirt, and when you lose it, you feel miserable, unhappy, beaten. You see how nonchalantly the others turn their heads and squeeze their nose between their fingers. You think it's gross. Then one fine day you're forced to do it yourself—until this foul habit becomes second nature. You've got over one of life's difficulties."

—

Lifting a shovel for nine hours a day is tough work. You can't make it mechanical: you manage three rhythmical movements, then at the fourth the shovel gets heavier, wobbles, and the earth falls back on your head. It's cold. You can't stay still, standing up without moving. You have to get back to work, not think of the hours still left, of the last crust of bread already eaten, of your numb, frozen fingertips.

"No one around?" I asked Thérèse, braced against the wind in her lookout position. Near me Violette was working wearily. I could see her purplish nose in profile under her cap; the contrast with her velvety, black, dreamy eyes was comic.

"Violette," I said, "do a dance. Go up where Thérèse is." Violette was one of our entertainments. Small, with the look of a little girl fresh from some finishing school where they teach you good manners, how to recite poetry for your mother's birthday, how to bake a cake for your father's, she was always in a world of her own. Hardly anybody talked to her: it would have been like going into a room without asking permission. And then everybody knew what they'd find in that room—a dusty old grandfather clock, rather sad, with a feeble chime, and then antique furniture in a wan light filtering through half-closed shutters.

"*Ah, les beaux jours!*" said the subdued chiming voice, "*les beaux jours d'autrefois*, when you went *chez maman* of a Sunday in your carriage and the road was smooth and straight under the clatter of the horses' hooves and the trees along the avenues flew merrily by with their tender new leaves . . .

157

How fine it was"—her voice went on with its feeble, monotonous ticktock—"baking *pommes de terre farcies*. My husband loved them so much!"

That was Violette, a small, fragile trinket of a thing with soft hands, half girl, half woman, beating eggs for a cake in the kitchen with her apron on or embroidering little handkerchiefs in the old armchair by the window—sweet, faded, limited.

She loved people to ask her things so that she could refuse, then give way. She climbed a little reluctantly onto the heap of sand. We all watched that little bundled-up figure; she looked as though she were made of rags, one of those toys that break as soon as you buy them. Her cap slipped to one side, her overcoat had been pulled tight at her waist with a belt of frayed cloth, and on her feet were a pair of small clogs. From her tiny hands dangled two enormous gloves made from some rough material.

All at once this rag doll came to life. Her feet lifted gracefully on her toes and her hands gesticulated in rhythm. After the first movements—who would ever have guessed—Violette was taken over by *l'humour*. Her black eyes became more languid above the purple nose, her cap jerked farcically, and the empty, floppy fingers of her gloves began a comic commentary on her singing and dancing.

The comedy won over her audience. Everybody laughed when Violette stopped and returned to her normal self, and yet they sensed that she had betrayed her nature in that performance, that there was something jarring and tragic in her comedy, for the dance had belonged to the *"beaux jours d'au-trefois,"* when Violette had danced it with impassioned grace and earnestness.

—

Tante Berthe had an absent expression about her: it was the day of the X-ray.

"So, Tante Berthe, did you see your son?" I asked her.

"Well, will you take a look at this," said Olga, winking, "haven't we dolled ourselves up today! Oh, Tante Berthe, I bet he loved you. You're such a darling in that kerchief!"

Tante Berthe laughed, flattered by the joke.

"I heard him before I saw him."

"How come?" we all said at once.

"Yes. The *Aufseherin* took me to the hospital in the men's camp. I had to wait in a sort of anteroom while my son in the next room was visiting his patients. I recognized his voice at once: my heart beat loud. 'Any moment now . . . any moment now,' I was saying to keep myself calm. When the nurse led me in, the room was dark. He took me over to the screen and asked me what was wrong. I could barely speak, but he recognized me and I felt him tremble. Then his hands found mine for a moment and squeezed them hard. And that was all. But in that instant, that furtive squeeze, I felt he put all his heart, his trust, his courage, his hope. The German nurse was there in the dark, and I was afraid his voice would give us away.

"He hesitated a moment, but when he spoke, in

German, he'd got his professional voice back. 'Considerable weight loss, generally run down, but no organs damaged.' The nurse turned on the light, his eyes fastened on mine, staring immobile, and in French he mouthed, *"Au revoir, madame, bonne chance! On reviendra en France!"*

———

The pit on the far side of the road was the most exposed. It was a large hole, almost exhausted now; the walls had been cut into terraces and the women worked with picks and shovels, passing the sand down from terrace to terrace, worker to worker, as far as the road where carts and big trucks came to be loaded.

All the prisoners working in the pits had been grouped together in the area where surveillance was easiest. Farther away was a line of loading trolleys. Beyond that the eye could wander over the immense plain, picking out the small villas built for SS officers and their families.

The sun had barely risen, was still pale and giving no warmth. There was no news, whether true or false, to talk about. It had been a while now since anyone had said *"Mes enfants, j'ai entendu dire que les Allemands . . . On est au bout . . ."*

"Tu sais, chérie, que les Anglais . . . ça c'est vrai, c'est plus que certain."

"What do you mean, you haven't heard? All the work parties are talking about it. Yesterday in the toilets I heard . . ."

It seemed the whole world had been plunged

160

into a desolate and tragic stillness, without voice or passion. Every movement of the shovel and every stroke of the pick was pointless and machinelike; like an insect trapped between smooth surfaces, your spirit slipped down and down, finding no hold, nothing stable. You might manage to think of nothing, feel nothing, but it couldn't last. Suddenly, you would find yourself trapped by the fierce grip of memories, and that was dangerous.

"You remember, eh, Giuliana," Madame Lea might say with her typical Belgian inflection. "how fine it was, combing their little heads?" And like a devouring cancer the nostalgic thought of my daughters would take hold of me, together with the vivid, tormenting sensation of the warmth of their skin, the softness of their curls. You felt at once the need to remember, to lose yourself in yearning, and at the same time the desire to suffocate every memory, to isolate yourself, harden yourself, become a dry, empty husk in the solitude of the sand pits.

"*Io ho un mantello neró!*" said Charlotte painstakingly. "The hell with these accents!" She was putting all the mental strength she had into her Italian lesson.

Raising her shovel, Olga made up the questions: "*Dov'è la carta bianca?*"

"*La carta bianca,*" replied the docile Charlotte, "*è sul mio tavolo.*"

Dawn was behind us, the two rawest, coldest hours behind us.

"Oh, *regardez mes enfants,* on the road . . ." said Thérèse, "a maid's going by with a bottle of

161

milk!"For a moment the shoveling broke off; all eyes were drawn to that once common, familiar object, a bottle, which had become so strange and exciting for us. And our eyes drowned in a whiteness that seemed to grow and grow, and to taste warm too, with a steamy smell of soft, buttered bread, heated rooms, sweet, childish feelings, the coziness of home.

"Milk!" our lips murmured or mouthed as if to say the word. All our throats were dry, our stomachs empty and cold, our spirits hopelessly miserable.

"Tu hai il cappello verde, io lo ho neró . . ." Charlotte went on with unusual stubbornness, but this time her words had the sound of someone talking without listening to herself, and anyway Olga had stopped paying attention.

Along the road that ran by the pits and parallel to the camp, some prisoners were dragging two carts loaded with white cabbages. Not all the women had seen them. Two or three of the Greeks working with the loading trolleys broke away from their group. Their wild instincts had sharpened their attention; they made up their minds fast, their spirits bold and consciences malleable. Thérèse likewise left our group, but none of the other French or Italians moved. There were no supervisors in sight, no *Posten*. The women ran cautiously at first, then faster, heads down. They reached the cart and each of them came back with a big cabbage under her clothes. Those who had stayed behind watched the adventure from a distance with bated breath. The cabbages were buried in the sand.

"Could you do it?" I asked Olga, and I felt how my own nature writhed and resisted; for as long as I lived, I would always rebel against the idea of plundering or stealing, never voluntarily expose myself to the justified humiliation of a beating.

"I couldn't," Olga said. "But not out of cowardice." And once again I felt spiritually tied to her.

Later Thérèse dug out her cabbage impatiently and passed me a leaf, saying, "It's amazing how sweet it is!" And while the tender leaves were squeaking between her teeth and her mouth was full of the sweet freshness of it, she added, "*Mes enfants, je vous jure:* when I get back to Paris and go by a greengrocer's, *je ne pourrai me tenir d'organiser un petit chou!*"

News of the stolen cabbages reached the camp authorities. That evening, after roll call, the *Sandgrube* party had to stay outside, in the cold, without eating, without resting, on their feet for two hours: *Strafappell.*

The camp was shrouded in darkness: the lights went on in the blocks and the other prisoners stretched out wearily on their bunks. Outside, in front of the blocks, a shuffling of clogs could be heard from the women standing in line. They were stamping their feet, hugging themselves, forcing hands deeper into pockets, but in their mind's eye each of them saw the smile of joy on their friends' faces as they savored the tender white leaves of the cabbages.

17

Christmas

When the siren woke us in the morning, all five of us hugged, without looking each other in the eyes. We stayed close to each other for a long time, each body seeking to soak up the warmth of its neighbors, arms linked, eyes half-closed.

Our hearts were in France and Italy, in the intimacy of our homes, with our loved ones. Remote childhood images rose to the surface with the charm of fairy stories—the shops full of goodies, festoons of small salamis, and baskets of dried figs, eels darting about in tubs, the faint sound of the bagpipes.

There Is a Place on Earth

Best not to think of it, not to spoil what few pleasures the day offered us: the sight, that is, from our warm beds, of the crust of frost on the windowpanes and the icicles hanging from the roof opposite, and then the anticipation of a bowl of goulash from which other hands would no doubt have taken care to remove every piece of meat before it got to us. All the same, it was enough to excite the stomachs of those who had had nothing but the same old wurst and margarine for ten months now!

The bunk below, Edith's bunk, was empty. Everybody loved Edith. Despite expecting a baby, her drained face beneath the flame of her Titian-esque hair had never lost its smile, her lips had never uttered a word of discouragement. Her features strained, body heavy, legs swollen and stiff from tiredness, she had shared the dust of the *Schuhkommando* and the cold of the sand pits with the others, never tried to use the imminent birth as an excuse for getting out of work.

At midnight Edith had gone to the surgery, transformed for the occasion into a delivery room.

She had started having contractions the day before, Christmas Eve.

A confused excitement reigned in the dormitory, a deliberate ostentation of merriment, with singing, dancing, and fooling around. The Greeks had formed a circle around three girls who chose pieces of clothing from the others to put together garish costumes for themselves. Those in the circle clapped their hands while the three figures in the middle did traditional dances or sang popular love songs in Greek and Spanish, with hundreds of impassioned voices joining in from the bunks above.

To the left of the door the French had formed a more disciplined group. They sang too, but softly— humorous nonsense songs about camp life, work parties, the *Boches*. And they recited poems; but when they moved on to traditional French songs, the girls' sense of humor was dampened and their voices grew husky with emotion.

The groups had formed out of instinct, with each woman trying to find in those around her a tiny piece of her own land and family.

Nobody but the very few who were close to her remembered Edith that day. Everyone had her own personal problems to deal with, the struggle between nostalgia and reality. Edith was ignored all day in a corner of the dormitory, behind the noisy partying women, between her bed and the window, stretched out on a hard straw mattress or sitting on a wooden stool. In her mind she had set up a sort of defensive line, beyond which the singing and squawking of seven or eight hundred people could not reach her. She was pale and she couldn't find a comfortable position. She lay down, hoping for some respite, but the pain forced her back to her feet; she sat on the stool and immediately, instinctively, her hands felt for something to grab hold of on the boards of the bed above, as another contraction seized her stomach.

In that corner of the dormitory, amid the deafening racket, Edith was alone. Her husband, if still alive, was far away in another concentration camp and unaware he was about to become a father; her mother either had been deported or was in hiding. Like every mother in this world, Edith didn't know if her child would be born alive or not, but what was more, she didn't know if her child would even be allowed to live or if he was destined for the crematorium as soon as he was born. She didn't know what she would cover him with, nor how she would feed him.

Toward noon we finally got the news: Edith was well. She had given birth to a beautiful little boy, weighing eight pounds; he had opened his eyes, wailed, and immediately closed them again forever. They put him in a cardboard box in the cellar.

The women went to see the baby, and were moved and said, "A beautiful little boy. It's better this way . . ." Or they said, "What a shame . . ."

I didn't want to see him. I wept, my head under the blankets, whether more for your birth or your death I don't know, my little baby.

All he wanted was a cradle with bows of ribbon, soft little cardigans knitted by Mama and Grandma, like every other child in the world. But the age of miracles is long gone. Likewise the Star of Bethlehem, the ox, and the ass.

18

Camp Show

I was coming back from work with my hands thrust in my pockets, weighing up the day's pluses and minuses.

"Another day of captivity behind me! Today wasn't too cold." I could still feel the warmth of the sun on my back; that blessing even the Germans couldn't take from us.

Many of the work parties were already back. The women had split up into groups around the tables or under the windows, waiting for roll call. I went to a table and took my last piece of bread from my pocket.

"Did you know," a Greek woman was saying to her friends, "this evening after roll call they're going to hang two girls."

"*Dios del mundo*, why?" asked another.

"Enough of these Greeks," I thought, "they're never happy if they haven't got a horror story to tell. They've been through so much they see the crematorium and death everywhere." Irritated, I got up and headed for a window where I could munch my bread in peace.

The siren for roll call had everybody rushing outside. There was a strange atmosphere, unusually solemn. Like black crows, the SS women stood wrapped in their cloaks. There was that general nervous tension that foreshadowed unpleasant developments. I looked at Olga; her face seemed to say, "Here we go." The roll call went on longer than usual. We were waiting for someone to arrive. Three male prisoners in striped uniforms walked ponderously by in front of our lines. The one in the middle was a giant of a man.

"The executioner," I heard someone whisper. A shudder ran along the lines. All at once a car drove fast around the corner and drew to a brusque halt behind us. The camp commander got out together with two or three others, who—from their uniforms and the way they walked—must have been big shots too.

"About face!" We reached an open space between the blocks. In the patch of sky between the two lines of still unlit blocks, the last flames of the

169

sunset were fading away. The evening's shadows fell from the roofs, and in the uncertain twilight flocks of crows flew low, cawing. Against the background of the sky in that staring twilight, we could see the silhouette of a gallows. A woman soldier, those unnatural beings that Nazi Germany had bred, herded us forward with threats and shouts like a flock of refractory sheep.

"The Union in the first row!" The place of honor was reserved for the party who worked in the munitions factory.

A lamp came on on the gallows and we could see two ropes hanging from the central bar; the figures of the *Lagerkommandant* and the prisoner-executioner stood out on the platform. A sudden buzz of activity and the crowd of prisoners drew back to let the victims through—two Polish-Jewish girls, barely twenty years old. They walked calmly, resolutely. After years in the camps, months of imprisonment, and exhausting interrogations, they had learned that in any event, one way or another, you had to die.

From the platform the German snarled: *"Sabotage . . . Sabotage . . ."*

The victims were accused of having supplied a group of prisoners working in the crematorium with the gunpowder that three months ago had blown up part of the building and made one of the famous gas chambers unusable, and then of having substituted the powder in the shells with earth.

"This is a crime against the Great Reich, this is

sabotage, and as such it must be punished by death," thundered the German.

Not for one instant did the officer realize what that accursed building meant to the prisoners. Ever since the first family had disappeared in the crematorium, ever since the mysterious room that filled with gas had swallowed up sisters, friends, and workmates chosen at random in the selections, we had watched the flame burn over the chimney. At first it burned only at intervals, then unceasingly, day and night. And ever since we arrived, that building had devoured our hopes, exhausted our energies, made the nights sleepless and dreadful, transformed the daytime into an eternal, nerve-racking death trap.

All the prisoners had their eyes on the ground, their faces tight; flashes of hate, horror, desire for revenge flickered across everybody's features.

When the figures of the victims came into the pool of light that shone over the gallows, a Polish girl broke out in a loud wail. She had recognized the victim as one of her prison friends.

"Shut up, or I'll send you to keep her company!" An *Aufseherin* was immediately on top of her, fists raised, and above the stiff uniform her ruthless face was alien to any emotion or female sentiment.

In the silence that followed, all I could hear was the sinister sound of my teeth chattering from shock and cold. The suffocated cry outside was echoed by another in a hospital ward; the sister of one of the girls was trying to throw herself down from her bed like a maniac.

The two Poles offered their delicate necks to the executioner. Overcoming his emotion and horror, the man, another Pole, gave the rope a determined tug, and two silhouettes looking tragically like puppets swung in the air as the stools were kicked away from beneath their feet.

The lamps went on around the barbed-wire fence. Outside, the noise of singing violated the deathly silence. In front of the camouflaged SS barracks, which the Germans had built identical to the camp huts to exploit the fact that the enemy wouldn't attack the concentration camps, soldiers were being drilled. They were parading up and down, singing, and, with stools on their shoulders, practicing the upright martial gait they were supposed to have under the weight of their backpacks.

The two silhouettes with their lolling heads swung in half-turns on themselves, their arms twitching against the starry night sky and the harsh light of the bulbs that etched out their shapes and shadows.

The soldiers' marching had stopped. We heard their roll being called, the names shouted in a military tone. In the darkness and silence they rang out like the names of the souls called to justify themselves at the Last Judgment: all guilty, all of them, from the *Lagerkommandant* himself to the most miserable *Posten,* guilty of the crimes committed in these camps of death and torture.

Finally, the prisoners were allowed to go back to their dormitories. By the barbed-wire fence, at the edge of the camp, was a fir tree, electric bulbs on its branches illuminating the coils of wire below, spreading a light that had neither warmth nor decency. It was the Christmas tree the Germans had brought to the camp for the festive season, when the memory of families and homes was most painful and poignant. "Of course," I thought, "the tree's still there. Tomorrow is Epiphany; today is the fifth of January!" And I felt a tenderness for that tree, torn away from its companions in its native forest, a prisoner like us, naked, without fairy lights or baubles or tinsel festoons.

Nature took pity and the next day, Epiphany, the tree was covered with snow.

Coming back into the dormitory, we all headed for our beds without looking at each other, exhausted. There was none of the normal chatter, the usual hum of voices. Each of us lay on our backs with our eyes half-closed; nobody touched their bread or sausage rations.

A half hour later the other work parties got back from work. Attempts to hide themselves in their beds or in the toilets were in vain. Two more victims were waiting to demonstrate to the other half of the camp that in Germany those guilty of sabotage would be punished on the gallows.

19

The
Voices Again

In the *Schonungsblock* in Auschwitz you could
recover from your flu without the fear of facing a
selection.

"There are no selections here," said the prisoners, "because the moslems and anybody with
anything contagious get sent to Birkenau." "Moslems" was the camp name for those who were no
more than skeletons.

Lying on my mattress, I abandoned myself to a
state of feverish drowsiness, my eyes half-closed.
From the background hum and movement that had
begun to animate the building, I guessed that the

parties were back from work. I wanted Olga to come and kept sneaking anxious glances at the door, which opened and closed with a light bang.

Finally, a white figure in her nightdress slipped furtively through the doors, looking around circumspectly, and decided to turn left, behind the beds, rather than strike out along the central aisle. Hugging the bunks, she was soon at my side. She lifted a mess tin by its handle and dangled it in front of my face.

"How are you, Giuliana? Eat, the soup's good today; we had some extra at work and I've brought it for you." I lifted my face and tried to smile.

Olga's face focused on me and darkened a shade.

"No thanks, love." I made an effort to sit up. "You eat it. I really can't, not today. I can't."

Her forehead furrowed into a grim frown.

"What do you mean, you can't? You've got to eat! You're weak, you're pale. You're paler than yesterday. You don't want to hold out, admit it, you're giving up."

There was a strange apprehension about her, as if I wasn't keeping my part in a pact we had made against death. And if one of us were to give up . . .

"It's the voices. They're worse than being hungry, worse than being cold," she said to herself, and I knew that by the voices she meant the call of the past, a mixture of nostalgia and memories, of desperation and death wish.

"Yesterday I felt so strong and I hoped I'd be back with you soon. The days are so long here

175

alone! It was last night that did it. I got up to go to the toilet. It must have been the middle of the night; from the window I could see the stars shining, and the blue light was on in the block. I was still more than half-asleep and I didn't want to wake up properly so I'd be able to get right back to sleep again. All of a sudden I turned and saw a young woman, tall, standing beside me.

"In that uncertain light, where every detail slips into shadow, I saw she was wearing a pale green *liseuse*. I woke up with a start. Mother's pale green *liseuse*, the knitted one with a flounce all around."

I fell silent, still shuddering at the memory. Olga listened intensely, holding my hand.

"All at once," I went on, "I felt the warmth and softness of the wool around my neck."

My mother-in-law had sent me the *liseuse* in prison so that I wouldn't get cold at night. I used to fall asleep with the wool around me to protect myself from the rough prison sheets. It was something from home, something that still had the smell of our drawers, soft as my own bed, warm as an embrace. I'd had it in my hands the whole trip from Italy to Auschwitz, where it was snatched away from me along with my clothes when we took our shower on arrival. That night I would have given anything to have had it back, even my bread and margarine.

"Mother's *liseuse*—and where is Mother now?" The eternal torment of these eternal questions, the torment of not wanting to resign oneself to an answer. Olga squeezed my hand.

"The *liseuse* was the last link between me and her in prison, and now it's come back, like a message . . ." My face in the mattress, I sensed that after giving me a last squeeze Olga had gone. The voices are terrible; they call to each other, they mingle with each other, they run after one another like notes in a fugue. Olga walked uncertainly toward the door, her mess tin swaying from side to side, as if she were hearing something too.

In the distance I heard the siren for *Lagerruhe*, silence.

20

Toward
the End

The war dragged slowly toward its final phase. One
sign in the becalmed life of the camp that things
were speeding up outside was that there was less
and less work for the prisoners. Many of the work
parties had been broken up or slimmed down for
lack of materials. The factories had less to do and
most effort went into getting the few materials that
were around safely back to Germany. Having been
quarried for years now, the sand pits were exhausted and could no longer offer work to hundreds
of women. The Germans were faced with the tedi-
ous problem of thinking up something new for us

to do, something that would be an appropriate form of persecution.

That day a group of women was taken off along the road that led to the village to work far away from the camp in the garden of a new villa.

"Look," said Olga, lifting the *Trage* full of earth, "that window over there with the thin blinds down. I can smell the warmth of an inhabited room, the warmth of the people who live there. The window-panes are fogged over . . . there's an embroidered cloth on the little table, with a jug of steaming milk on top, a slice of cake left on the plate next to the knife . . . Somebody's been knitting in the armchair in the corner, the ball of wool's fallen on the floor and the little cardigan is blue . . . My God, to be able to sit on a chair . . . I've had enough of nine hours a day digging and shifting earth, I can't stand it. And to be able to eat with a fork . . . my spoon always tastes of tin! But I can't see the Germans living in there, I can't see them."

"Yes," she went on, narrowing her eyes. "and on the other side there's the bedroom: a smell of soap and lavender, of clean linen folded in cupboards. I can smell the freshness"—she shivered, passing her shiver on to me too—"the freshness of laundered sheets around your body."

"And the people living there," I said, "don't even appreciate what luxuries they enjoy—drinking water and breathing air—people who don't know what war means."

"Look over there, in that corner of the garden, a

toy wheelbarrow," Olga went on. "There must be a
baby." She broke off when I said, "I don't want to
see it. I don't want to see it!" The memory of my
daughters obsessed me; I didn't even want to remember their faces anymore.

A man and a woman came slowly along the road,
arm in arm. He bent lightly toward his partner; she
lifted her face toward the young man, taller than
she as he walked by her side. Neither Olga nor I
spoke: our deepest beings were shaken by a shudder of amazement at the sight of this incomprehen-
sible reality, by the sharp pain of having once been
women.

Coming along the road to meet the couple from
the other direction was a baby carriage with small
wheels, and it was open. A woman's hands leaned
confidently on the steering bar and her body bent
forward as she pushed her little cargo. Again my
body, my arms, my back, remembered the position,
at once familiar and strange.

"The baby, no," I said to Olga, "the baby I can't."
It was the image of all our little ones the gas had
choked in their mothers' arms not far away from
here. For the first time I felt I was capable of hatred
and the tears froze in my eyes.

—

It was no good asking worked-out pits to fill trolleys
and carts with sand. There was no more work for
the women in the *Sandgruben*. Along the fence that
divided off the assembly shops and workshops at-

tached to the camp, there was an open space, and
the Germans decided to develop it as soon as possible into a grandiose avenue with a raised strip of
grass all down the middle and flower beds, lawns,
and paths on each side: a *Volksgarten*, they said, a
public park. One morning the *Sandgrube* party thus
became the *Strassenbaukommando;* we set out
from the camp gate and turned left rather than right.

The sky was still muted and empty, and lights
were still shining at the crossroads where the various tracks met. Beyond the hut with all the tools
lay the work area, framed by the frost-white
branches of trees. The ground was white too, and
when your shovel lifted the snow, amazed at its
lightness, it was to lay bare a stony soil the frost had
made hard as marble. Sparks shot from the pick and
the first shovel thrusts were destined to fail. The
sun came up. First it was a thin, curved strip
spreading a crescent glow, then, to our admiring
eyes, it grew superbly round and climbed above the
narrow strips of dense cloud that tried to waylay it
so that as the sky was kindled, light streamed down
in luminous bands between one cloud and another.
The rapture for your eyes was to dazzle yourself by
looking into the source of light through half-closed
eyes, then turn at last to open them on the pale rose-
tinged faces of your companions. Polish dawns,
dawns without expectations, the pick growing
heavy in your hand or a shovel under your arm.

Farther off a party of men were working, a lot of
them French, some Italian, all ashen and starving.

Amid their striped backs, a dry, nervous figure appeared and disappeared. He wore a black jacket,
and a pink scarf around his neck, and the muscles
in his face searched for a tough, violent expression.
The supervisor of both parties, men's and women's,
this German wasn't at ease with the women; he
didn't trust his facial muscles quite enough, and so
he preferred to harass the men far away, a little out
of sight of the women, kicking them in the shins
and the backside, punching them on the nose and
jaw. People fell, got to their feet again, their faces
smeared with blood dribbling from their nostrils;
they cleaned themselves and stooped lower over
their work.

"A garden," the women said, "a park, just a few
months before the end!" For nine hours the shovels
rang on the gravel and the stones slipped uncon-
vincingly into the hollows to level the ground. We
had already raised the strip along the middle for
quite a way, slightly arched, promising to become a
green *pelouse.*

Working apart from the others, Julian and I were
heaping together, then carefully distributing, piles
of soil, banging it down with our shovels to make it
smooth and flat. The supervisor who didn't trust his
facial muscles had chosen a Dutch farmer as *Vorarbeiter* to check on the women.

*"Est-ce que tu te rappalles, Julian, de la loi du
pendule?"* I asked my French neighbor while I
tried to dispel the mist in my brain. "And in what
way does it relate to Newton's law?"

What hard work: more so than lifting the shovel

or beating down the hard earth. My dull brain, deprived of phosphor, struggled like a paraplegic trying to get to her feet. Yet something still shone in that darkness; above all there was a never-forgotten thirst for culture, the craving of the still-unextinguished spirit that made us suffer in hopeless attempts at concentration but that also distracted us from the empty, monotonous rhythm of the shovels, the vision of hundreds of futile mechanical beings.

"Oh," shouted Julian suddenly, "*pense tu*, Giuliana, I've remembered the formula for ammonia: NH_3!"

"Giuliana?" asked the Dutch *Vorarbeiter. "Wer heisst Juliana? Heissen Sie Juliana?"* He looked at me.

"Ja"—I smiled—*"und sie auch Julian, die Französin."* I nodded to my friend.

"Wie eure Königin," said Julian.

"Wie meine Gattin," whispered the man. *"Was glauben Sie? Krematorium?"* Taking the heavy iron wheelbarrow from Julian's hands, he set off in a stumbling walk without waiting for an answer.

The following day Julian had a small piece of white soap to use in the shower; in my pocket I hid a small box of Dutch vaseline to grease my cracked lips with.

—

Five *Kübel* of soup instead of three! Five *Kübel*, neatly lined up, almost double the normal ration.

"Look, five *Kübel*, two of them 'organized' in the kitchens!" the women whispered, smiling.

"How come?"

"See that big Polish guy, striped pants, blue jacket? He's important, escorts the men who take the *Kübel* to the kitchen. He's got a *kochana*, a lover, here in our party, a Polish girl. 'Organizes' the *Kübel* for her and the whole party."

We were waiting timorously in line behind the *Kübel*, eyes never leaving the big ladle as it dived again and again into the drums, pouring out their contents into the mess tins. Steaming tin between stiff fingers, each woman looked for a corner where she could crouch down and eat.

One open *Kübel* still not quite empty steamed in the icy air; another beside it hadn't even been opened.

The women ate slowly, in silence, right down to the last spoonful. Farther away the men huddled together, bent over their tins, carefully scraping out the bottoms.

Then we got patiently into line again. The ladle rose and fell rhythmically, another half tinful.

"For the men—they've eaten less than us, they can barely stand."

And each of us set out, holding our tins in trembling hands.

"Careful now," the women said to each other. "A little bit for everybody, no favorites."

"They mustn't argue over a few spoonfuls of soup."

Everyday at the same time the men, their tins still dirty from their own soup, sneaked over to our group.

"*Madeleine*"—Thérèse was reproachful—"*il ne faut pas la donner toujours au même.*" She added, to the others, "Always to the same French boy, nice but not very thin. Look at that one; I'm going to take mine to that ghost thing there." She ran off with a nervous jump and the graceless movements of her woodenish body.

"Look," I said to the *Vorarbeiter,* "my tin's under that bush. Take it over there to somebody who hasn't had anything."

My soup wasn't to have a face; it was for *him,* who had certainly had nothing and could eat nothing.

Suddenly, with the mess tins still scattered around on the ground, the air-raid siren began to wail. Men and women ran back to their lines while thick white plumes of artificial fog rose at regular intervals from the guard towers along the perimeter fence and spread out in the air. In just a few moments the landscape was lost in it; people could barely find each other; every now and then the branch of a tree might loom out, or a patch of ground. Your throat and nostrils were stinging, and the smell of the gas made you feel nauseated.

As though in a milky sea, the prisoners were strangely lost; every reference point had gone—camp, huts, barbed wire.

him. I called him over, and you know what he said? 'I don't want it, Mama. Take the other fifty back too. I like to want candies. I'll say, "I want some candies," and you go and get them for me.' "

Sara was happy: beneath her modest face she had her ideal world.

"What do you do in Belgium?" I asked, impressed.

"We emigrated from Bessarabia. We have a newspaper kiosk in Brussels."

Behind a workshop a group of men prisoners had lit a good fire.

"Let's go over a moment and get warm," Sara said. "Two minutes every trip."

"What did you do?" a tall youngster standing next to me asked in German; he was a political prisoner from Poland.

"Where?"

"Before coming here, of course."

"Well," I said, hesitating, "I taught Latin and Greek." And immediately this seemed absurd and I felt ashamed, as if I had told a lie.

"Aha." The Pole laughed, incredulous. "You mean you were going to school yourself! You can't be more than eighteen, you! *At regina gravi iamdudum saucia cura vulnus alit venis et caeco carpitur igni . . .*" he began to recite. In his mouth the Latin took on a strange, harsh accent.

"*. . . solus hic inflexit sensus animumque labentem impulit. Adgnosco veteris vestigia flammae,*" I picked up.

There Is a Place on Earth

"Ah, Virgile!" Madame Sara sighed. *"J'ai fait mes études littéraires en Russie!"*
Everybody around fell silent. For a moment everything had vanished; there was only the heat of the fire slowly seeping into our clothes and the echo of the Latin poetry that had united three people of different nationalities and tongues inside the barbed-wire fence.

A large sugar beet was roasting over the fire. A woman watched over it and inhaled its aroma. It was almost cooked.

"Get that junk off the fire!" warned a big Pole who had come up close.

"Just a moment," begged the girl, "it's nearly cooked."

"Get it off, or I'll chuck it away." The woman didn't move. She didn't believe such an absurd threat. But the man grabbed the beet by one end and with savage speed threw it on the ground and smashed it three, four times under his shovel.

She gazed at her squashed, inedible beet. She couldn't even find anything to say in protest.

"You filth," I screamed, "you're worse than the Germans!"

The man had acted out of racial hatred. Despite having been subjected to the same atrocious conditions, the same spiritual sufferings of the concentration camps, these anti-Semites still felt the Jews owed them something.

I picked up the bricks I had put down.

"You can stay," said the tall Pole who had recited the Latin.

"No, that's the end of that," I said and went off.

—

Coming back from work, our party stopped at the entrance to the camp. A group of women were coming out of the main gate carrying suitcases.

"The 'rare birds' are off to work," whispered Olga.

That they were rare was clear enough. Each woman's cheeks were daubed with great round blobs of rouge, her lips transformed into voluptuous curves of red lipstick, the whole face generously sprinkled with an overly white powder. Tight dresses left the legs bare above the knee, swaying on very high heels. All of them had beautifully soft jackets of splendid white mohair.

Sometimes they would waft about the camp, crooning some song under their breaths along the perimeter fence, their brazen laughter bringing white teeth and red lips into sharp contrast. The other women stopped and stared, and saw that despite all the show these girls, like themselves, were imprisoned by the camouflaged buildings and barbed-wire fences.

"*Bordell siebzehn!*" said the *Oberaufseherin* during evening roll call, calling out the name of the party of voluntary Aryan prostitutes along with those of all the others.

Of feminine seduction, grace, and attraction the

camp could offer only the miserable artificial substitute of uniformed prostitution.

"They're not even thin," said Olga. "They get enough to eat, they do."

Three *Kübel* instead of five means starvation again if you're working outside; when the thermometer slips to fifteen below, a minimum of calories are required. Thus begins the hunt for extra soup, or rather for the anonymous leftovers in the mess tins. But there is a block in the camp where whole drums of soup are left untouched and where the women, almost all Polish, sit at their tables listlessly stirring the stuff in their tins and tasting only a spoon or two with a grimace of disgust. In front of them they have margarine canapés with sugar, plus carrots and slices of bread and dripping. So if you manage to sneak as far as their quarters, maybe you can get a ladle of soup. But the ladies here are pretty aloof: because it's rather annoying having your meals interrupted by the scroungers from the *Aussenkommando.* These camp aristocrats are those who work in the parties that give them every opportunity to "organize": like all privileged classes, they are the only ones who can afford to feel disdainful or disgusted.

When hunger rages, the scroungers get aggressive; but it's obscene, this begging for soup, and the doors of the block are closed. Next day the full drums are poured away down the toilet.

21

Bread, Patience

For some time there'd been no more air-raid warnings, day or night. Only two or three planes had flown over the camp that morning, but the German officers had stopped to look at them with unusual attention.

"The Russians are near!" The rumor came from the men's parties.

"Oh sure they are!" answered the women, incredulous after months and months of hopes, illusions, and disappointments. "Four months ago they were only forty miles away." And some added ironically, "In a couple of months' time . . ." No one wanted to give up the indifference and imperturbability that had been so hard-won.

The lights went out in the dormitory. Amid the last vague muttering I heard Madame Paul's voice from the bunk below: *"Cette nuit peut-être . . ."*

Unsuspecting, the prisoners slept, refusing to get excited, banishing the unsettling thought of imminent liberation.

Someone dashed up the stairs and into the *bloccova*'s cubicle. A quarter of an hour later the lights went on in the dormitory, and the supervisor's voice announced that various parties would be setting out in the morning on foot.

We dived out of bed, stunned. Here at last, bursting into the desolate, gray monotony of camp life, was the certainty that events were speeding up.

Our hands lingered on our blankets, our eyes gazed around the dormitory and then, dazed, came back to our companions. This end we had dreamed of was still so mysteriously fraught with risk and disappointment that we couldn't enjoy it.

Images of relatives far away assaulted hearts and minds exhausted by emotion; and for those who set out toward a terrifying unknown, departure from the torture camps became itself yet another painful leave-taking from families, homes, and native countries.

"Roll up a blanket, everyone roll up a blanket," said Olga, desperate to be doing something practical so as to calm herself down.

The night was a succession of roll calls and in-

Giuliana Tedeschi

spections; but at dawn the sun rose confidently, promisingly, and the biting air galvanized the prisoners' nerves.

The camp gates opened for the last time. Heads up, stepping out determined, aware that every moment was taking us farther from the camp, and forever, we could sense the distance growing behind us, though we didn't look back. Outside the fence and the blocks the sun struck us head-on; after the night's tension everybody's face began to take on an incredulous smile. When we were far away and had reached a bend in the main road, I turned and stopped to gaze at the landscape.

Spread out in the middle of the white plain from which trees rose stiff and gaunt, in a blaze of snow that sparkled in the sun, sharp against a clear blue sky, lay the silent, beguiling Auschwitz. Far away on the horizon was the village, dominated by the thin spire of the church, the only testimony to village life and normal human existence that, thanks to its height, the Germans hadn't been able to keep from us. In front of the village were the red-brick buildings, soiled and saddened by gigantic daubs of camouflage paint. They might have been papier-mâché, an unnatural superstructure imposed on a countryside where otherwise the winter landscape and the village with its old church and sloping roofs would have fused together in beautiful, traditional harmony.

"Look at them, they look like papier-mâché," I said to Olga, pointing. "They must have been mined. They'll fall flat on the ground like a child's house of cards." We turned in silence to continue our march. From that moment on, we had left Auschwitz forever; our hearts turned eagerly to the future now, and the future was freedom. We hurried forward by leaps and bounds, like sheep let out of a pen.

"What's happening?" I asked my neighbor all at once. "There, yes. They've stopped; they're milling around on the edge of the road!"

Halfway along the column, lots of women were rushing and slithering into a snow-covered ditch beside the road.

"I can see something like a wooden shed," she answered, narrowing her eyes.

"*Brot, Brot*—bread, bread!" we heard them shout. A big cart, its drawbar bent, had fallen from the road onto the grass beside and lost its whole load in the snow. The loaves, in the classic loaf-pan shape, lay in little piles or were scattered here and there across the snow, as if spilled out by some gigantic cornucopia.

The women leaped onto them, each grabbing as much as she could carry, arguing and even fighting over loaves, sometimes ferociously. A piece of bread meant life for a few days more, it nourished the strength needed for the march, and above all it put hope in your heart.

The ancient Bible stories, whose miracles had fascinated me in infancy, then bred disbelief and doubt in adolescence, now came back to mind.

"Bread, patience . . ." went the popular proverb. Struck by the extraordinary nature of the event, I did not take any bread.

—

The column is getting longer; there are other women marching behind the Auschwitz group. The Birkenau women, thirteen or fourteen thousand of us on the road in all.

Will those we left behind be among them? Natalia, Dina, Ruth, and all the others? No, many women were sent by train to other work camps in Germany months ago. Then Dina and Ruth . . . we must consider them lost; they have watched the others leave—everybody who could stand on their feet, that is—with indifferent, almost extinguished eyes. Now they are lying on their mattresses amid the empty bunks in the disorder of the hospital block that still shows all the signs of flight and evacuation. They expect nothing.

The women have been marching since dawn. They have to stay in line to one side of the road; to the left, at regular intervals, are the *Posten* with their rifles slung across their backs, and a few *Aufseherin;* there are some women from the *Polizei* too with revolvers in their belts. Some have already overtaken the column on a wobbly cart, apparently looking to escape amid the general flight.

We have done twenty miles and the sun is nearly down. The landscape remains stubbornly the same —a flat plain stretching endlessly away under the opaque whiteness of sky and snow, deadening the already exhausted senses. The Germans accelerate their pace, not allowing us any more stops. Perhaps there is some goal to reach? How many miles away, when? Or perhaps this march is to be infinite, without a break, without a goal? By now our legs move only from the force of momentum. The road is littered with blankets, since many women, exhausted by the effort, have decided to abandon them. You're unable to lift your eyes to the sky; they remain stubbornly fixed on the ground, fascinated by the movement of the legs in the row before you, all advancing with the same rhythm—feet in clogs, feet wrapped in rags and strips of blankets, feet poking wretchedly out of torn shoes.

Earlier on, in the sunshine, everybody had tried to keep their eyes on the progress of their friends. Some had pressed ahead to the front of the column, others had lost ground, and Violette, her nose even purpler than usual, eyes swollen with tears, could scarcely move her swollen legs

I said something to her as she walked alongside me; when I looked for her a few moments later, she was gone. The road had swallowed her up. In the morning five pairs of hands would reach out to help anybody who slipped on the ice; in the evening those who slipped lay where they fell. No one had the strength to do anything but push their legs forward, and even this was automatic, not willed. You stepped slightly to one side so as not to trample on the body you found beneath your feet, and you went on without looking.

The moon came up, the landscape became

197

ghostly. The wind howled in the dense pine woods; it slashed your face, cut through your thin clothes and into your bones.

Came the echo of the first rifle shots fading away in the silent trees. We stopped, hesitant, listening, then, as if spurred on, dragged ourselves forward.

"Olga . . . Vicky . . . Giuliana . . ." Every so often we would call to each other in the dark, check that everybody was there; God help us if the bond of resistance that united us were to snap!

By now Violette, the mother of a small French girl, and others likewise who hadn't been able to keep the pace, were lying on their backs on the ground, black shapes in the whiteness, a small stream of blood trickling away in the snow.

Finally, to the right, against the plain we saw the shapes of a group of farm sheds! The sheds where we were to spend the night huddled and crowded together.

—

The dawn sun finds us already on the march. Those who lost each other in the dark rediscover their friends with joy in the morning. Already used by other columns of prisoners, the road is no more than a filthy bog. The Germans' luggage rolls by, the Red Cross vans. Defeat is in the air! A column of men catches up with our own. They're from Auschwitz too. They quicken their pace in response to the yelling of the Germans, overtake us, head off down a path through the woods.

There Is a Place on Earth

"The Sosnowitz men . . ." I ask, "have you seen the Sosnowitz men?"

"Yes, yes," one of them answers, "they're behind us." He hurries away.

My legs are trembling; I catch myself almost falling over. "Maybe I'll be able to see him," I think. "I'll be able to see my husband for a moment as he goes by, hear his voice in a greeting of hope." And I put a piece of bread in my left hand to be ready to offer it to him when he passes.

Nothing. The miles go by, not a soul in sight apart from our sad herd. But here and there, by the side of the road, in a ditch or a short distance away on the snow in the fields, lie bodies in striped uniforms. Those who feel their will to survive fading summon up all their remaining energy with a shiver of terror and loathing.

The front isn't far away. At night a glow of flames lightens the sky, and we hear the echo of bombs and artillery. The third day, flagging and disheveled, we ask ourselves, "How many more days now? Where to?"

Again and again, desperate cries of *"Pause, Pause!"* are raised, like the moans of someone on his deathbed.

Toward noon there are signs of confusion. The column sways, breaks up, comes to a halt.

"Wagons, wagons!" At last a cry of hope reaches our ears.

Ahead of us are a line of hills and at the foot of them the railway. Three tracks are occupied by sev-

eral dozen open cattle cars. We have reached Los-
lau, the German border.

The wearisome process of loading us on lasted
several hours and did not restrict itself to that in-
genious and universal formula of rail transport:
"Eight Horses = Forty Men." Instead it was,
"Eight Horses = A Hundred Women. Anything not
to walk another step!

—

As you climb on, you have the impression of at last
discovering in the plank floor of the wagon a stable,
immobile resting place. After so many miles the
earth seemed to move of its own accord, or rather it
seemed to impart movement to the legs of those
walking over it. And now it was the earth, dear God,
the earth that was running beneath us, while our
legs enjoyed the sluggishness of rest!

Being in a group of a hundred is still better than
being in a group of many thousands: the uniformity
of those huge numbers makes you nauseated. After
the disorientation brought about by the lack of any
sense of territory, the small box of the wagon comes
to mean safety.

Yells and shoves were followed by a sort of satisfied, relaxed truce. But soon your legs began to suffer; they refused to stay curled up or crouched and
were continually seeking some small portion of
nonexistent space. During the day it was totally impossible to maintain any kind of general equilibrium, and as night fell our bodies became nothing

more than a groaning tangle of heads and legs with mess tins and clogs sticking out here and there. Oh, the inaccessible wide-open spaces of the sky, the fleeting silhouettes of the trees standing out against it! Every limb was bruised, every bone ached, every mind was dark. Exasperated, the mass of bodies became bestial or mad and in this hell conflicts of race, class, and character exploded violently. Even prison friends, those who in tacit alliance acted as anchors to each other, had moments when they were overcome by bestiality, when they shouted their resentment, anger, and intolerance, and accused each other of selfishness and meanness, even though they knew that the bond of friendship that sustained them was far more important than any immediate need.

"Scum!" said the Italians and French, looking with sullen eyes at the more numerous Aryan Poles —sitting against the sides of the wagon, drawing on centuries of anti-Semitism, they kicked and punched away the rest of us so as to be able to stretch their own legs full-length.

—

At night the space seemed to shrink.

"*Lass mich meinen Platz nehmen!*" shouted Vicky, on the verge of tears, to a young Pole who refused to budge so much as an inch. "*Lass mich, verfluchte Polin!*"

In a flash the Pole was on her feet going for her eyes. She tore off her glasses and the two went down on top of each other over the legs of other screaming prisoners, fighting hard to hit each other, to get back the lost place and the lost glasses.

"Hässlich, blöde," Vicky sobbed, shaking. *"Ohne Augengläser bin ich wie blind!"* Her fist grabbed at a clump of hair of this girl who had smashed her glasses out of spite. When Olga saw she was going to lose the battle, she came to her aid and, eyes staring at the Polish girl, took a knife from her pocket, gripping it menacingly in her hand.

"Ow, ow," yelled Tante Berthe at the other end of the wagon, "they're sticking needles in my back, bitches, *verfluchte Bande!"* But the Polish women kicked her away, shouting, *"Weg, Franzuska!"*

Restless, the older women would lose their places and then with mad stubbornness simply sit on the stomachs of the others, wailing and cursing.

"Enfin, Tante Berthe, levez vous . . . vous m'emmerdez Madame Paul." No one was surprised to find herself screaming. In the fierce struggle for life there was no place for respect or generosity. And the *Posten* watched over this shrieking mass of humanity with alienated or feckless eyes, dealing out rough justice by bringing down their rifle butts at random on our heads. When the sun rose again to discover your wretchedness, a compassionate neighbor would use the snow that had fallen on clothes and blankets to clean away the crusts of blood congealed in your hair.

When shapes began to emerge from the dark, when it became possible to distinguish legs from arms, mess tins from heads, Olga yelled, "My mess tin, where's my mess tin? There was still a piece of bread and margarine in it!"

In our utter wretchedness the mess tin was a treasure. You sat on your mess tin, you slept on your mess tin, you clutched your mess tin frenetically to your breast. If you lost your mess tin, you were beaten; there was nothing left but to resign yourself to imminent death. Olga found hers under the legs of a big surly Pole. One weeps on rediscovering one's mess tin . . .

"*Herr Posten, Herr Posten,*" shouted Tante Berthe, her voice hoarse.

Her face was disfigured and ruined by dropsy, her eyes dull and distant. Constantly fighting with the Poles, who wouldn't give her even the tiniest space to sit, she protested to the *Posten.*

"You, *alte Huren,* let her sit down!" shouted the *Posten.* It wasn't one of the brutal ones that day, but a coarse young easygoing type.

"*Du, Französin, kannst du singen?* Can you sing the way Frenchwomen sing?" he asked, turning to Tante Berthe with a mocking tone.

With a bundle of rags in her lap, kerchief lopsidedly knotted under a haggard, exhausted face, she didn't realize he was trying to humiliate her. She opened her mouth: a labored, asthmatic voice squeaked out the first lines of a nineteenth-century love song in strained falsetto.

She gasped, she couldn't go on, and in her desperation at not being able to win over the German, she began to excuse herself. Yes, in her time she'd been a good singer, played the piano too. Of course she'd been different then, worn smart clothes. In her house . . . in France, she said, and she raised her voice noticeably in a tone of dignity and condescension.

Olga, Julian, and I lowered our distressed faces. To profane one's home and real life like this in front of a German . . . Her words certainly suggested an unbalanced mind.

"Leave her be, *Herr Posten*. I'll sing you a nice Italian song." It was the only solution I could think of on the spur of the moment to put an end to his derision.

"She's mad," Olga whispered to Julian after looking at me hard. "She's mad. We're all mad."

I made an effort; I summoned up my strength and sang an old song from Abruzzio, something I'd always liked for its rustic grace.

"Tu tene 'na vucchella . . ."

I was amazed to hear my own voice. It was toneless, metallic, distant. I could find neither abandon nor joy in my singing. Those ruined, brutalized faces were ranged mutely about me, while in the background the rumbling wheels of this spectral wagon headed toward the unknown.

"You, Italian, sing us another song!" insisted the *Posten* when I'd struggled to the end. Oh no, old friend, I wasn't singing for you and I'm not going to sing again.

There Is a Place on Earth

On a white board illuminated by a searchlight, we read RAVENSBRÜCK. After three days and nights the ghost train stopped. We got off in the dead of night and were arranged in rows of five again. The clashing of a gate behind us, a German voice counting.

Charlotte says we must be in Bavaria, because the houses glimpsed through the dark were all low villas with sloping roofs. There must be splendid woods all around. Instead we were in Mecklenburg, in a *Straflager* built in a hollow and surrounded by high walls. From the roof of the blocks hung icicles almost a yard long. The camp is like all the other camps that embellish this country; the only difference is the perimeter wall that robs us of any view of the green countryside. Indeed, it's so high we feel we've climbed down into a tomb, and an overpopulated tomb at that! Naturally, there's no room for the women from Auschwitz; the camps are all full to bursting, since the dead have been replaced with great ease. We are thrown out on the paths between the huts, hungry, thirsty, numb.

The only thing we get to touch in the huts is the floor, and not lying down but crouching. Heaps of us are locked in the *Waschraum*, huddled in round baths beneath trickles of water.

A Hungarian, a skeleton of a woman, filthy and disheveled, crouching near me, looks at her shirt and crushes something between her nails.

"Weg, Schwein!" the others shout with disgust, shrinking away from each other as best they can. Hopeless. The first flea is among us; two, three days

and everybody is scratching, studying their clothes, and crushing things between their fingers.

Everybody's morale is noticeably lower. The camp kitchen steams twenty-four hours a day. Your soup could arrive at any time of night. The cart with the soup *Kübel* stops in an open space in another part of the camp. The group of four whose turn it is to transport it hurry over. The *Kübel* are heavy and perched high up on the cart. You have to be strong and fast. There are cries in the dark, curses, people calling to each other. Maybe a *Kübel* tips over, boiling hot. When with an effort you've managed to lift your *Kübel* down, two tall, dark shadows detach themselves from a corner of the hut, heads wrapped in shawls. They are the Ukrainian marauders: goodbye, soup! They have "organized" your *Kübel* and they carry it off at a run. You don't eat, you hardly ever eat, and when you do, it's only after enormous efforts or beatings.

Then in the blocks where there are Aryan German women, the Jews don't eat at all, because they have no right to eat, and to make matters worse they can be robbed of anything they have with them, anything that takes the fancy of a blond tavern Valkyrie. Roll calls can go on from six in the morning till noon on the big central road: they're called *Strafapelle* (punishment roll calls), and everybody asks, "*Strafe* for what?" Then there are the inspection roll calls when they search us inside out and we lose combs, teaspoons, penknifes, belts, woolens, and mess tins. They serve as a pastime, since time is the only thing that is not in short supply.

There Is a Place on Earth

It takes half an hour's lining up in the cold to get into the toilet hut! Yet despite everything, faces go pale, hands clench, bodies shrink at the mere cry of *"Juden antreten!"*

Every day the Jews are made to line up for several hours, before a few hundred women are escorted away. Where to? To do heavy jobs? Dig trenches, shift rubble?

—

After Ravensbrück, Malchow is paradise. You sleep on pallets on the ground, you wash in washbasins, and you don't work, since there is no work, not even for the work parties who have been toiling for years in the munitions factories hidden in the forests. But by now the women are no more than ghosts and hunger is the only master. The bread ration is barely an inch thick, the soup is down to a pint of unsalted, tasteless water with a couple of turnip slices floating on top! There are periods as long as twenty-six hours without anything to eat. Your main occupation is saving energy and lying down.

Before setting out for the toilets you take your pulse and listen to your heartbeat.

In the silence at roll call you frequently hear the thud of a falling body. As soon as the lines break up, Bianca, the Auschwitz doctor, who as luck would have it was sent to Malchow before us, runs to help. Her movements are quick and confident; as before, she has a professional, dignified manner, but a furrow forms on her austere forehead.

"Nothing. Pulse very weak," she says. "We'll lay

her head down on a piece of sloping ground to get the blood back to her brain."

From beneath the eyes a yellowish puffiness spreads out over the fainted woman's face, and beneath the pressure of our fingers the skin sinks and turns white.

"Dropsy," says Bianca. "It's the first symptom."

—

Prompted by starvation, a mania was going around the camp, an obsession with recipes and imaginary meals; it had become pathological.

"Meat ravioli," said Bianca, sitting on my mattress, and the whites of her eyes seemed to expand. "Then . . . sole fillets with mayonnaise."

"No," another woman interrupted. "What about roast beef with crisp, salty fries . . ."

"Oh . . . voluptuous hunger!" said Bianca. "It's as if I could already taste it—"

"Enough!" I yelled, getting up from my mattress. "Stop it, or I'll slap your face. Your hunger may be voluptuous, but mine's raging, okay? It's worse than exhaustion, worse than semiconsciousness. My guts are in knots, my stomach is killing me, I can't feel anything else, I can't think of anything else. When you talk about food, I turn into a beast . . . Bianca, I'd rather we talked about pulmonary tuberculosis . . ."

I hurried out of the block toward the toilets. The speed of the first few steps almost made me lose my balance, and my trembling legs gave me the impression my heels were lower than my toes.

There Is a Place on Earth

"Dis donc, tu te rappelle, toi, de la soupe aux haricots blancs?" Two Frenchwomen were absorbed in their powwow by the door to the toilets.

I ran on; I took refuge in the toilet, closed the door, and passed my hand over the hollow of my empty stomach.

—

A heavy-framed woman hurried into the block, walking quickly and circumspectly to the area where the Russians were. Under the jacket of her striped uniform she was hiding something pretty bulky. Fast and furtively, she placed her find under her pallet and called her companions.

A while later the youngest came back with a big stone. Out from under the pallet came an enormous bone, an animal's thigh bone, stripped bare of its meat, a treasure taken from the garbage pile of the SS kitchen. The strongest of the Russians took the stone, another held the bone still, and the rest formed a huddle around them. After numerous blows the bone finally gave way and disintegrated.

Crouching with their heads in their shawls and a piece of bone in their hands or laps, they looked like ghouls around a carcass. They chanted a song —first just big Natasha's clear warm voice, then the others in chorus. It was a nostalgic song, full of echoes of a distant land, boundless and seductive, a never-ending steppe under the snow, crisscrossed by troika tracks.

A group of Frenchwomen listened, ecstatic; in

209

front of them were mess tins full of potato peel that had been carefully cut into small pieces and mixed with green-onion tops, together with a pinch of rock salt to taste.

—

Given that Malchow was certainly the less threatened area, why in early April the Germans should have sent half of the prisoners to Leipzig must remain forever a mystery.

By this time the Leipzig camp was constantly being shaken by bombs and artillery fire; in fact one wing of the main building had been damaged by the bombs.

The besieging forces closed in; they were only a few miles away; the Germans hadn't given us any bread for five days.

The atmosphere in the camp was one of overexcitement and nervous expectation.

"Vous allez voir," said the French, who were always the first to give way to enthusiasm. *"Cette nuit ou bien demain . . . Bientôt en France . . ."*

The order to evacuate came suddenly, toward ten in the evening. By eleven we were on the road again, in the thousands. And we were marching east, back to the Russian front.

Thousands and thousands of prisoners from different camps were wandering around in a now limited area of about forty miles, and it was getting smaller every day.

Oh, woods crossed at night when our eyes lifted

to the tops of the trees, begging our freedom of a cold, indifferent, star-studded sky!

And the drone of the planes flying over us in raid after raid! The noise seemed to come out of the most hidden nooks and crannies of the thickets to swell inside us along with our heartbeats.

The gloomy landscape persecuted and oppressed us, instilling a continual sense of peril, ambush, and death.

At dawn the first road signs showed that we hadn't left the Riesa area. The march had been a sham; the reality was that we were surrounded. We slept out on the roads and in clearings; every wood was full of people. Bodies collapsed exhausted on the stony earth or damp soft grass, shivering from cold and fever. Every hope of being fed was gone and the women got down like grasshoppers at the edge of the fields where small tender broccoli plants were growing or in the meadows where already-blooming sunflowers offered their leaves and the hearts of their buds.

But even after ten days of fasting, marching, and cold, lifting a clod to take a seed potato was still a crime of such gravity that a *Posten* might simply finish you off with a bullet in the head.

"Oú est Tante Berthe?"

"Oui, Tante Berthe s'est évadée ..." The news passed along the line at the beginning of the day's march. We were worried and afraid.

"Thérèse aussi," a friend added three days later. "She couldn't walk anymore. She went into the

door of a German house as we were crossing the
town."

"Oh my God, what will become of them?" everybody wondered.

The afternoon was drawing to a close. A thin rain
had been falling for hours, soaking our clothes, and
now an icy wind was freezing the wet material on
our bodies.

The road was one puddle after another, the
meadows sodden with water; there was no shelter
for our exhaustion. A light fog settled on the land.
Nature herself seemed to have deserted us, wanted
to swallow us up into her own sadness. Our hearts
were arid and mute; every capacity to react was
fading. Hunger and weakness had reduced us to
skeletons. Every physical reserve had been used
up; we didn't have even the strength to talk.

Having arrived at the Elbe, the column came to a
halt. We stood around for hours without knowing
why, sodden with rain and tormented by the cold.
As night fell, the rumor got about that the bridge
over the river was down and we would have to wait
for dawn to cross.

The temperature had fallen, shoulders ached,
teeth chattered. I took shelter by a wall with four
other friends. I could feel life gradually slipping
away from me, and my fears grew. I had the very
clear sensation that I was close to the "final solution." After months and months of suffering and
every kind of moral and physical torture, it was terrible now to feel that freedom was so near and to be

desperately afraid of not having that last ounce of strength still necessary to survive!

A profound regret, which went beyond any feeling of affection or family tie, a regret for life itself, filled me with a sweet emotion. There was a progressive detachment from existence; it went on step-by-step, without any more traumas now, as my physical strength faded away. And yet the world, emerging purified and new from this gigantic tragedy, would be a better place, must be a better place, must reward our yearning for perfection, our thirst for improvement, so that the martyrdom of so many not be in vain. I want to live because I need this new world, I need to feel myself born again!

Night dragged on. The destruction of the bridge had stopped the prisoners from going any farther. Other columns caught up with us and scattered around the area.

It was like a miracle. In the midst of the tramp of heavy footsteps passing on the cobbles, we suddenly heard the familiar sound of our own language. Voices from Alpine Italy, the slithery tones of the Veneto, resonant southern dialects, even more welcome for the immediate vitality of their vernacular. "Italians, Italians!"

Figures came out of the dark and one after another stepped into the light cast by a nearby lamp. The faces appeared for a few moments, and as they did so we anxiously looked for and joyously recognized the features of our own people. The nearest stopped amazed: three Italian women in the midst

213

of a never-ending column of Poles, Hungarians, Russians, French.

"Listen, for the love of God, we can't hold out anymore. We haven't eaten for ten days and we've been walking all the time. Have you got anything you could give us?"

"No, nothing," someone from Trieste answered. "Except for a few potatoes . . . raw."

We trembled; perhaps all wasn't over just yet.

"Oh yes, please," our voices quavered. "Raw potatoes . . . if only." The young man came back with a treasure trove—nine raw potatoes and heartfelt fraternal sympathy. He was sorry he had nothing else, he said, neither he nor his friends; he was upset to see women from his country in such a bad way. We were all moved and hugged each other. Crouched on the ground, we sliced the nine potatoes, dividing them into five equal parts.

No sooner had the few raw slices quieted our exhausted stomachs than we had the idea of escaping, running off from the Germans. In a few minutes the idea became a concrete decision for all five of us. Fearful and excited, we tore our numbers and camp emblems from our clothes. We found another group of Italians, disbanded soldiers, and decided to link our fate to theirs.

The night passed. At dawn the SS and the *Posten* gathered together the column to cross the Elbe. Hearts beating fast, we didn't move from our hiding place. All the men set out in search of food. They lit a fire, made us sit down and get warm while pota-

toes cooked in the mess tins. We ate without peel-
ing them. We trembled, our hands too impatient
and feverish.

"Eat, eat slowly," they said. "We'll always have
enough now, don't be afraid!"

Meanwhile the whole column of prisoners had
gone on. By now it was clear that nobody was looking out for us anymore. The time had come for the
Germans to look out for themselves. Across the
river streamed a never-ending line of trolleys, carts,
and vehicles of every kind, prams with crying babies, flushed mothers with children and bundles in
their arms, men dragging enormous loads of household belongings. The German civilians took prece-
dence over us, of course. All day we waited in vain
to be able to cross. Then we realized they had
blown up their munitions dumps. We took refuge in
a cellar for the night; it was the last of our captivity.

All of a sudden the sound of artillery fire. For two
hours the house was shaken by explosions. There
could be no doubt: we were in the midst of the
battle! We heard distant confused shouts, hurrahs
perhaps. Shortly afterward a soldier on horseback
stopped by the steps down to our cellar. "Germans
or Russians?" he asked. No one answered. It was
still dark; we couldn't make out who or what he
was. When the firing stopped, someone went out
and came back shouting, "The Russians are here!
We've been liberated!"

We were incapable of any emotion whatever. All
sensibility had been paralyzed, our minds numbed;

every excitement would have to be postponed. The men brought us the first food relief. "Bread, bread!" And in the dark, without even realizing it, we ate jam and salami, sugar and liver paté, biscuits and bread, all mixed up, amazed by so many different tastes, which for us fused all together into a single, insatiable voracity.

With the first light of dawn we went out. Where the evening before hundreds of German civilians had been standing waiting to cross the Elbe, now there were only overturned carts, food, clothes, pots and pans strewn over the ground, open suitcases, gutted chests, garments and underclothes sodden with slime. Most of the people had fled, many had been carried away by the river, some lay dead. Here and there were the corpses of soldiers and horses, empty cartridge cases everywhere.

We hurried across the battlefield to get to the Russian army quarters as soon as possible. We took a road across the fields; then, finally, I turned round.

No more barbed wire, no more nightmarish marches in rows of five, walking behind other people, seeing their legs move in front of you, knowing you were followed close behind by other legs. Oh, to be master of the road, to be able to walk sideways, in the middle of the road, on the edge, able to stop, turn, shout: "Free, free at last!"

It wasn't sunny; the sky was gray. As the image of those corpses strewn across the ground, their faces turned up to the sky, came back to me, as I recalled those shreds of domestic life tragically abandoned, plundered, and spoiled, those fragments of an absurd, mad, perverse humanity, I turned and took refuge in the light dawn mist.

A few Russian soldiers going by waved cheerfully: *"Ah, italianke, charasciò."* We looked at our liberators, men ethnically different from us, rough-and-ready, but spontaneous and friendly too, and in a hybrid language made up of *russki, charasciò, spassiba, gut, italianki, Gefangene,* we tried to express our gratitude. When feelings are overflowing and the circumstances are so special, you don't need words to make yourself understood.

Then, from the distance, a group of officers approached.

"French uniforms!" shouted Julian. A captain of the French medical corps together with other officers was coming over to the prisoners to offer assistance. She flew to him and threw her arms around his neck: *"J'embrasse en vous la France, monsieur!"*

It was then that something broke inside us. The emotion, at first anesthetized, then held back, put off, mixed with fear, erupted in tears and moans of joy. We all embraced, at last convinced of our liberty.

About the Author

GIULIANA TEDESCHI was the wife of an architect and the mother of two children when she was deported to Birkenau in April 1944 by the fascist government, which was paid five thousand lire for every Jew turned over to the Germans. Though she returned from the hell of the camps, neither her husband nor her mother-in-law did. She eventually rebuilt her academic career and spent forty years teaching in the same high school in Turin. She is the author of high school texts for Latin and Greek, a manual of Italian grammar and usage, as well as other texts in ancient history and geography. Now retired, she lives in Turin.